# Effective teaching and learning

i

A(R)

# Effective teaching and learning

*Teachers' and students' perspectives*

*Paul Cooper*
and
*Donald McIntyre*

Open University Press
*Buckingham • Philadelphia*

Open University Press
Celtic Court
22 Ballmoor
Buckingham
MK18 1XW

and
1900 Frost Road, Suite 101
Bristol, PA 19007, USA

First Published 1996

A catalogue record of this book is available from the British Library

ISBN   0 335 19379 X (pb)   0 335 19380 3 (hb)

*Library of Congress Cataloging-in-Publication Data*
Cooper, Paul, 1955–
    Effective teaching and learning : teachers' and students'
perspectives / Paul Cooper and Donald McIntyre.—
        p.    cm.
    Includes bibliographical references and indexes.
    ISBN   0–335–19380–3 (hb.). — ISBN   0–335–19379–X (pb.)
    1. Teachers—Great Britain.   2. Teaching.   3. Learning.
4. Teacher–student relationships—Great Britain.   I. McIntyre,
Donald, 1937–   .   II. Title.
    LB1775.4.G7C66   1995
    371.1'02'0941—dc20                              95–19491
                                                      CIP

N371·102
410964

Typeset by Graphicraft Typesetters Ltd, Hong Kong
Printed and bound in Great Britain by
Biddles Ltd, Guildford and King's Lynn

# Contents

# Acknowledgements

The research reported in this book was supported by the Economic and Social Research Council as part of its Research Initiative on Innovation and Change in Education: the Quality of Teaching and Learning. We wish to thank the Council for its support, and also the Steering Group of the Initiative, led by John Gray, the coordinator of the Initiative, Martin Hughes, and our fellow researchers in the other nine Initiative projects. We wish to thank our colleagues in the University of Oxford Department of Educational Studies, Chris Davies, Hazel Hagger, Louise Harvey, Anna Pendry and Richard Pring, for the many and varied ways in which they helped with this work, and also Jim Mitchell of the University of Canberra, a very pleasant, thoughtful and helpful collaborator during his study leave with us. Most of all we want to thank the schools, the teachers and the pupils who so graciously gave their cooperation and time to the research, and who made their expertise accessible to us.

# 1/ *Exploring classroom strategies for effective teaching and learning*

This book is about how teachers and pupils try to teach and to learn effectively in classrooms. It explores their understandings of effective teaching and learning as these inform and are reflected in their classroom practices. It goes on to examine the ways in which teachers' and pupils' strategies reflect common or conflicting concerns, and how they work more or less effectively together to promote the pupils' learning.

These concerns with what teachers and pupils try to achieve in their classroom work, and with how they try to achieve these things, offer an important perspective on the work of schools. Most obviously, any serious attempts to improve the quality and effectiveness of teaching and learning in schools must start from an understanding of what people in classrooms do at present. More specifically, the initial and continuing professional education of teachers needs to be informed by understandings both of how experienced teachers do their work and of the ways in which pupils set about their classroom learning. Similarly, the curriculum frameworks within which teachers are asked to plan and conduct their teaching, and the assessment and reporting frameworks through which both teachers and pupils are held accountable for their work, will be sensible and useful only in so far as they take account of how teachers and pupils do their work and of why they work as they do.

Sadly, these rather obvious truths are not always recognized. The quality of the work of schools, and especially the effectiveness with which pupils learn and are taught, have in many countries become increasingly important and contentious political issues in recent years. In Britain, for example, politicians' dissatisfaction with the quality and effectiveness of schooling has purportedly been the reason for radical changes in the nature and structuring of school curricula, in the assessment and reporting of pupils' attainments, in the management of schools and in teacher education.

There has certainly been no shortage of complaints from the politicians about what is done and achieved in schools, or of recipes for reform; but these complaints and recipes have not been based on evidence about what does happen in classrooms, and especially not on well-grounded understandings of what teaching and learning strategies teachers and pupils adopt and why they do so. The politicians have been quite rightly concerned with what they would like done and achieved in schools; but since their imposed innovations have not been based on an informed understanding of what people do in schools and in classrooms, there must be considerable doubt as to whether these innovations will produce the desired results.

It is ironic that, as politicians seem since the 1960s to have become increasingly confident in their prescriptions for schooling, those whose task it is to study classroom teaching and learning have become increasingly conscious of the complexity of classroom life and of the difficulties of making helpful prescriptions for it. Until the 1950s, research into teaching tended to be of two kinds: 'methods experiments', in which the relative merits of different overall recipes for teaching particular subjects or topics, or for managing classrooms generally, were compared; and explorations of the personal characteristics of 'the good teacher'. By the 1960s it was increasingly recognized that teaching could be neither described nor prescribed for in terms of anything so simple as standardized methods, that good teachers could be distinguished only by their teaching, not by any kind of distinctive personality profile, and that to understand teaching one needed to study *what happens* in classrooms. This recognition of the need for extensive classroom observation was complemented in the 1970s by a growing realization that to understand teaching one needed not only to see what teachers did but also to get access to their classroom thinking and decision-making. Even then, researchers were over-ready to believe that they understood classroom teaching and to import theoretical models based on false preconceptions. In 1986, Clark and Peterson, in an authoritative and influential review of research on teachers' thinking, concluded that their own and others' attempts to develop models of teachers' classroom decision-making

> may have been premature . . . We would suggest, therefore, that before specifying a new model or revising the existing models of teacher interactive decision-making, researchers should first do more descriptive research on how teachers make interactive decisions.
>
> (Clark and Peterson 1986: 278)

The history of research on classroom teaching has thus been one of a gradually developing understanding of its complexity and of the blind alleys which await those who are too ready to make assumptions about the nature of teaching or of effective teaching. And while, during the 1980s and 1990s, there has certainly been a great deal of interesting and valuable research into teachers' thinking and classroom activities (reported, for example, in Halkes and Olson 1984; Ben-Peretz *et al.* 1986; Calderhead 1988; Day *et al.* 1990, 1993; and in the journal *Teaching and Teacher Education*), it is of course less easy to see the blind alleys of the present than those of the past. That there is, however, a continuing temptation to conduct such research from within frameworks of prescriptive theorizing about teaching is apparent in a good deal of recent research, for example that which (deriving largely from the work of Schön 1983, 1987) assumes that good teaching is necessarily 'reflective practice'. On the other hand, there may also be a contrasting temptation, in view of the disappointments of the past, to abandon any concern with the effectiveness of teaching.

The dominant model of the 1970s for research into teaching effectiveness was the *process–product* model, at the heart of which was the examination of correlations between *product* measures of, for example, desired pupil attainments and selected *process* measures of classroom activities hypothesized to be conducive to these desired outcomes. At least in European contexts, this approach to the study of classroom teaching has largely fallen into disuse, partly no doubt because of the practical difficulties of conducting such research in ways that take account of the known complexities both of classroom processes and of the desired outcomes. The virtual collapse of this tradition has, however, left a void that remains to be filled. We do not claim that the work reported in this book fills that gap, but we do see it as a useful step on the way.

The way forward must be one which recognizes the dangers of making assumptions about what happens in classrooms or what effective teaching involves and which takes as its starting point the attempt to understand what people in classrooms are trying to do, and how they go about trying to do it effectively. There is no suggestion here that the people who work in classrooms already know all about effective teaching and learning, but three things *are* suggested.

1 First and most important, the things that teachers and pupils try to achieve in their classroom teaching and learning, the ways they try to achieve these things and the problems they encounter offer very fruitful starting points for generating hypotheses about effective classroom teaching and learning.
2 Only through knowing about teachers' and pupils' classroom practices and the thinking that underlies them will it be possible to theorize incisively about the *limitations* of current classroom practice.
3 Only through knowing about teachers' and pupils' classroom practices and the thinking that underlies them will it be possible to educate beginning teachers or to plan curricula or in other ways to plan intelligently for the development of classroom practice.

In starting from these premises, the research reported in this book is not an isolated enterprise, but is instead able to build on previous work. In particular, it builds very directly on previous studies of teachers' *professional craft knowledge*. From the mid-1970s, scholars in both the United States (e.g. Lortie 1975; Ebel 1976; Cohen 1977) and Britain (Desforges and McNamara 1977, 1979; McNamara and Desforges 1978) began increasingly to question the use of social scientific or other 'external' theories as appropriate starting points for seeking an understanding of classroom teaching. They suggested that teaching might usefully be viewed as a 'craft', and that a fruitful way of seeking to understand teaching would be to gain access to, and thence possibly to 'objectify', the knowledge implicit in teachers' everyday practical classroom activities. The craftsperson analogy has been further elaborated by, for example, Tom (1984), in *Teaching as a Moral Craft*. The power of the analogy lies in:

- its expectation that each individual will have a distinctive expertise, although it is none the less probable that some features will be common across teachers;
- its emphasis on knowledge which is embedded in everyday practice;
- the idea of the craftsperson being able to analyse specific situations, to draw upon an individual repertoire of craft knowledge and to apply it appropriately in context;
- the possibility of an experienced craftsperson being able in large measure to communicate his or her craft to a willing learner.

Our use of the analogy does not imply any further preconceptions about the knowledge that guides teachers' classroom practice. Teachers of course do have other kinds of knowledge, which they use for other purposes, and their craft knowledge is likely to be more or less integrated with the totality of their professional knowledge; but it is with their professional craft knowledge, the knowledge that informs their everyday classroom teaching, that we are especially concerned.

The research reported in this book builds especially on that of Brown and McIntyre (1993), a Scottish study that was a first attempt to explore in a very open way the nature of individual teachers' professional craft knowledge. It is to that study and to the ways in which we sought to build on it that we now turn.

## Building on the Scottish Study

*Making Sense of Teaching* (Brown and McIntyre 1993) reports a study which aimed 'to explore the professional knowledge and thought which teachers use in their day-to-day classroom teaching, knowledge which is not generally made explicit by teachers and which teachers are not likely always to be conscious of using' (p. 19). In particular, the aim was to explore the nature of 'good teaching' in the context of one city secondary school and its feeder primary schools, focusing on the last two years of primary school and the first two years of secondary school. The 16 teachers on whom the study focused were selected on the grounds of there being some consensus among their pupils about strengths in their teaching, and of their availability and willingness to participate. 'Good teaching' was defined as what was seen to be good on the particular occasion by the individual teacher and his or her pupils. Of the 16 teachers, four were primary school teachers and the other 12 were from ten different subject departments of the secondary school.

Each teacher was observed for a 'unit of work' of between two and six hours, and was interviewed about the observed teaching after every lesson and again at the end of the whole unit. Since the aim was to gain access to knowledge that teachers were unlikely to be accustomed to articulating, care had to be taken to achieve this, and to ensure that it was the teachers' own authentic accounts of their teaching that were articulated, not ideas fed to them by the researchers. The strategy that was used by the researchers to achieve this involved, in summary:

- emphasizing what was good about the teaching, in the eyes of the teachers and their pupils;
- focusing on specific classroom events which occurred when both teacher and researcher were present;
- determinedly avoiding the imposition of any researcher preconceptions about good teaching or about how to make sense of teaching;
- helping teachers to remember what was involved in doing the things they did well, the most important element in this being to interview the teachers very soon after the observed lessons.

The study revealed a rich diversity of concerns and practices on the part of individual teachers, but the researchers also sought to formulate and to test generalizations that were valid across teachers. The main generalizations are summarized in Figure 1.

The teachers studied all evaluated their teaching in terms of their attainment of *normal desirable states of pupil activity*, which are steady states of activity seen by teachers as appropriate for pupils at different stages of lessons, and *types of progress*, including pupils' learning or development, the creation of products and the coverage of work. Both the standards used by teachers in setting their standards for evaluating how well their goals were attained, and the teachers' selection of appropriate actions from their generally extensive repertoires, were strongly influenced by a large number of circumstantial conditions, of which the most salient were those relating to the pupils being taught.

The picture of teachers' ways of making sense of their own teaching

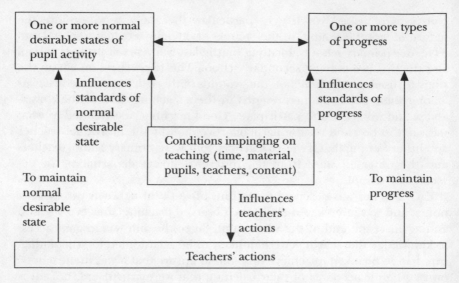

*Figure 1*  The concepts that teachers use in evaluating their own teaching. *Source:* Brown and McIntyre (1993: 70).

that is given in Figure 1 is not only very abstract but also a significantly oversimplified account. In a more intensive study of the practice of five of the 16 teachers, the researchers found that

> these teachers rarely took single actions to attain single goals [and that there were] various ways in which combinations of actions, sequential or concurrent or both, chosen according to diverse conditions, [were] used to attain one goal or possibly more than one goal; and . . . some circumstances in which the actions which teachers found necessary for attaining two different concurrent goals were mutually incompatible, so that the teachers were obliged to concentrate on their more important goals.
>
> (Brown and McIntyre 1993: 106)

It was as a direct follow-up of the Scottish study summarized above that the research reported in this book was planned. The Scottish research seemed to have given a very clear and positive answer to the important question of whether, given a suitable approach, it was possible to gain access to teachers' professional craft knowledge. It had also provided a very useful broad initial picture of the nature of teachers' professional craft knowledge. Inevitably, however, it left a large number of questions unanswered. Those which were of primary concern to us in the present study were as follows.

The first was *generalizability*. The Scottish conclusions were based on the practices and thinking of only 16 teachers in one Scottish secondary school and its feeder primary schools, with classes of 10–14 year-olds, in the late 1980s. How similar would the findings be in another place, at another time and in different circumstances? In particular, how similar would be the craft knowledge used by teachers in England, coming to terms with the National Curriculum?

The second was *elaboration*. The Scottish study had deliberately investigated the professional craft knowledge of teachers teaching a wide variety of different subjects and at both primary and secondary stages. Given such a design, there had been no opportunity to consider the extent to which differences and similarities among teachers reflected the subjects they were teaching, and far less the subject curricula they were pursuing or their individual understandings of their subjects. What similarities and differences would be found in the craft knowledge used by teachers teaching the same subject curriculum to pupils of similar ages and abilities?

Similarly, the Scottish study had deliberately selected teachers because of their diverse strengths and therefore it was not surprising that the aspects of their teaching that they had focused on were very varied. Would it be possible to map out the nature of teachers' craft knowledge more fully if one concentrated on particular facets of their teaching?

It was because of such considerations that the research reported in this book focused on teachers of only two subjects, English and history, and on their work with year 7 classes within the National Curriculum; and that it was especially concerned with the subject teaching aspect of the teachers' work and with their ways of taking account of differences among the pupils in their classes. The choice of these two particular subjects was to some extent arbitrary, but was also influenced by the fact that research on the teaching of these subjects, even more than, for example, mathematics, science and modern languages, has been very limited.

The third question was regarding *pupils as actors in the classroom*. The Scottish study attached considerable importance to pupils as people in a position to judge the merits of teachers' classroom teaching: pupils' judgements played an important part both in the selection of teachers and in providing feedback to teachers on the observed lessons. The investigation was, however, unambiguously about teachers and their teaching: it was *their* classroom thinking and activities that were the focus of the research.

However, just as research on effective teaching in the past neglected teachers' thinking to its cost, so at equal cost it neglected pupils' thinking. Increasingly, research has demonstrated the need to study pupils' classroom thinking as a determinant of the effects of teaching upon pupils' learning. For example, research studies have demonstrated the importance of pupil perceptions in mediating teacher expectancy effects (e.g. Cooper and Good 1982), pupils' reported attention, motivation and specific cognitive strategies in mediating the effects of teacher instruction (Peterson and Swing 1982), and pupils' attributions in mediating the effects of classroom success and failure (e.g. Dweck *et al.* 1978). It was therefore decided that the research to be reported here should focus not only on teachers' professional craft knowledge but also on the mental activities of pupils that by their own reports lead to successful learning; or, in other words, on the classroom learning craft knowledge of pupils. This additional focus was planned to enable us, furthermore, to attend to the 'bi-directionality' (Shavelson *et al.* 1986) of teachers' and pupils' classroom influences on one another.

In the remainder of this chapter, we shall briefly outline some of the background, in policy, theory and previous research, to these particular new foci in our research, complementing the general concern with teachers' professional craft knowledge. This will be discussed under the four themes of:

- the National Curriculum context: background debates;
- the craft of subject teaching/pedagogical content knowledge;
- taking account in the classroom of differences between pupils;
- the classroom craft knowledge of pupils.

## The National Curriculum context: background debates

An important aspect of the context of our research was the controversy that surrounded the introduction of the National Curriculum at secondary level, especially in relation to the two subjects, English and history, on which the research focused. Little (1990), in a contemporaneous discussion of the Final Report of the History Working Group, describes three areas of debate: professional, academic and political.

A major focus of debate was, and continues to be, on the selection and organization of subject content for presentation to pupils. In both English and history professional educators in schools and institutions of higher education were debating (and continue to debate) which parts of their subject should be included in or excluded from syllabi. The professional element of the debate is concerned with issues of pedagogical appropriateness and theories of teaching and learning, the academic element is concerned with ideologies about the nature and purpose of the academic disciplines of English and history, and the political element in the debate deals with questions of cultural and social empowerment (e.g. *whose* English and history are to be endowed with high status by being prescribed in the National Curriculum and to what purpose?).

At the root of the contentions surrounding selection is the issue of selection criteria. The polarities of this debate are neatly summarized by Collicott (1990: 8) in her paper on the final report of the history working party, when she asks on behalf of primary school teachers:

what knowledge is suitable for the diverse populations in our schools[?] . . . what knowledge is suitable to prepare children for a pluralist society? . . . Do the programmes for study for Key Stages 1 and 2 fit with the child-centred and topic approach of good primary practice? Do the programmes offer a body of history knowledge that is relevant to our children?

Collicott's comments indicate something of the wide diversity of contextual variables that help to shape one view of 'appropriate' subject matter. Collicott suggests that the History Working Group, in its final report, ignored the social and cultural context of teaching and learning, and in so doing undermined teachers' opportunities for teaching history effectively:

There is a direct relationship between how a teacher organises the learning in her classroom and how she selects what knowledge to present to children. Both aspects need to be based on the needs and experiences of the child and, we must remember, the children in our schools draw on diverse backgrounds and experiences.

(Collicott 1990: 8)

Collicott argues that the historical content that is prescribed in the programmes of study is essentially ethnocentric because of the emphasis it places on British history. This ethnocentricity is detrimental to the aim of educating pupils from diverse ethnic backgrounds in ways that encourage them to value their own cultural origins and those of others who are not of white Anglo-Saxon origin. Furthermore, Collicott sees this effect as being incompatible with the 'child-centred' pedagogy that she (citing the support of HMI) equates with what is widely accepted as good practice in primary school history teaching. The implication of her argument is that in order to operate a child-centred approach effectively one must engage with pupils' understandings and values at the content level rather than simply 'instruct' them about a content that is divorced from their daily reality.

Slater (1991) agrees that the History Working Group's report is overly prescriptive, and like Collicott he objects to the form of pedagogy that he believes to be implicit in this approach. The heavy prescription of content, he believes, denies teachers the opportunity to employ pupils 'as resources' (Slater 1991: 16). He is referring here to the use that creative teachers can make of pupils' existing historical knowledge, going on to suggest that it is precisely through this harnessing of pupils' existing knowledge and interests that teachers can facilitate pupil motivation for and engagement in learning.

Common to the arguments posed by Little, Collicott and Slater is the idea, articulated most clearly by Slater (1991: 15), that the National Curriculum as conceived by the History Working Group inhibits teachers in the exercise and development of their 'professional talents'. It is here that the main underlying theme of the professional debate is located. The major positions in the debate are best conceived in terms of two contrasting models of the relationship between the curriculum and teaching professionals. Each model implies a distinctive conception of the teacher role.

The first is *the National Curriculum (NC) model: the teacher as pedagogical expert.* The NC model sees the curriculum in terms of a body of knowledge and a set of values that should be prescribed by subject experts and delivered by teachers. In this model teachers' professional expertise lies in their ability and knowledge in the field of curriculum *delivery.* The selection of content is not the business of teachers. In this model the teacher is therefore seen as an expert in the restricted field of pedagogy, whose role is to develop the pedagogical strategies that enable expert knowledge, generated and selected by expert scholars, to be transmitted to students.

The second model is *the Educator model: the teacher as scholar and critic.* According to this model the tasks of teaching and of making final decisions about the curriculum are indivisible. It is therefore of central importance that teachers should have the subject expertise and the capacity for critical curricular thinking needed to decide what should be taught. Guidance from expert scholars can be welcomed but the final judgements must be left to teachers. The reason for the indivisibility of teaching and curriculum decision-making is that what is to be taught cannot be completely separated from to whom it is to be taught and how it is to be taught. An important aspect of making appropriately sensitive curriculum decisions is responsiveness to the immediate situation in which teaching and learning are to take place. This involves interaction between teachers and pupils as a basis for generating the curriculum (see Barnes 1976), so that teachers can take account of pupils' experiences, understandings and concerns as they become apparent. The teaching and learning model implied here stresses transactional interaction rather than transmission. Teachers are seen as needing considerable control over the subject content in order to engage effectively in the teaching process, since these cannot be separated from one another.

These two models reflect certain aspects of the typology devised by Ball and Bowe (1991) to describe subject departments' initial responses to the NC orders. They describe two main categories of response: (a) implementation and (b) interpretation. The implementation orientation corresponds to the first of the models described above, and is characterized by a willingness to adopt the prescriptions of the NC without question – a policy which Ball and Bowe found to be a source of difficulty when schools encounter contradictions and inconsistencies across NC documentation. The interpretation orientation corresponds to the teacher as scholar/expert model. This is characterized by a critical and reflective response to NC documentation, a willingness to challenge some NC assumptions and a mission to incorporate or appropriate the NC in terms of pedagogical and subject ideologies that are already held.

In English the early professional debate bore many similarities to the history debate. Two major areas of contention arose in relation to the content of the English NC: these concerned prescriptions about literature, and the use of Standard English. A third, and eventually critical, concern was with the proposed assessment arrangements for Key Stage 3. Teacher-critics of the English NC complained that the list of prescribed texts was by the nature of its inclusions and exclusions contrived to convey the superiority of a literary tradition that is dominated by white, male, middle-class English writers (Cox 1991). Similarly, the prescription that Standard English be taught to all pupils raised questions of social and ethnic discrimination (Hackman 1993), as well as arguments about the linguistic ambiguities surrounding the concept itself (McArthur 1993). As in the history debate, arguments against what were seen as a culturally biased curriculum drew on scholarly sources in the English studies field and were countered by references to opposing traditions.

Later, the opposition to the English NC would focus more on criticism of the notion of progression in language development implicit in the design of the curriculum, and pedagogical implications of the proposed content of tests (Barnes 1993). The idea that the tests would be knowledge based was seen as incompatible with 'the prevailing ethos of English teachers', which saw 'learning [in English] as personal . . . provisional' and 'recursive', and as such not available to 'snapshot testing' (Hackman 1993). This particular line of resistance challenged what was seen as a conservative impetus behind the NC, which it was thought would have the effect of enforcing transmission styles of teaching in English classrooms, and of replacing the preferred practice among English teachers (as advocated by the influential National Association for the Teaching of English (NATE) and the authors of Language in the National Curriculum (LINC) materials), which drew on theories about the active and participatory nature of learning, with practices reflecting a view of learning as a passive process (Hackman 1993).

In summary, arguments surrounding the initial introduction of the National Curriculum in English and history were greatly concerned with issues of curriculum content. Resistance to the new curricula was based on different perceptions of effective pedagogy and learning, different views of the nature of the subjects and concerns about the social and political implications of the content chosen. One major issue involved an opposition between a view of teachers as scholars with an active role to play in the selection of knowledge and a view of teachers as having the task of delivering a curriculum designed by others.

The research reported in this book was undertaken mainly in the year 1991–2, the first year of implementation of the National Curriculum in secondary school history teaching and the second year of its implementation in secondary school English teaching. Our exploration of teachers' craft knowledge was therefore undertaken at a time when teachers were in the middle of coming to terms with the implications of the National Curriculum for their classroom teaching. What impact this might have on the craft knowledge they used, or on the way they used it, we did not know. In particular we did not know to what extent, or in what ways, the kinds of ideological debate outlined above would impinge on teachers' classroom practice, on teachers' awareness of their practice or on the explicitness of the thinking informing their practice. What was certain was that we needed to understand the classroom teaching in the contexts of the teachers' understandings of, and reactions to, the National Curriculum they were being required to implement. We had learned too, especially from the work of Ball and Bowe (1991), to anticipate that these contexts might in important respects be *social* contexts, with debates within the subject departments and action taken at the departmental level potentially having a major impact. Our exploration of these contextual issues is reported in Chapter 3.

**The craft of subject teaching**

The idea that teaching expertise is to a very substantial degree expertise in teaching specific subjects is very well established in Britain, at least in relation to secondary school teaching. The dominant pattern of secondary school organization into subject departments gives an autonomy to these departments which implies that not only curriculum content but also pedagogical expertise are matters on which those who are not subject experts can make only very limited informed judgements. The same assumptions are reflected in the ways in which the initial professional education of secondary teachers is organized. It was therefore something of a surprise when Shulman (1986), in a presidential address to the American Educational Research Association, complained about the neglect of what he labelled 'pedagogical content knowledge' – those aspects of pedagogical expertise which involve taking account of the content of what is being taught. Perhaps this was a problem only on the western side of the Atlantic.

More careful reflection, however, made it very clear that in relation to Shulman's primary target, *research* on teaching, his assertion of a 'missing paradigm' was as valid in Britain as in North America. Subject considerations had, with very limited exceptions, been severely neglected in research on teaching, with the result that our analytic understanding of what is involved in subject teaching was very limited. In relation to history teaching, for example, Pendry (1994: 8) could find no British research on the nature of teachers' expertise and commented:

The articles in *Teaching History*, the only journal published in this country specifically for and about history teachers, are testimony to the extensive knowledge, skills and abilities of history teachers; but these remain unexamined: they are described but not analysed . . . the descriptions alone tell us little of how the teachers know what would interest and motivate their pupils; how they were able to make use of what they knew to create what seem to be appropriate activities and tasks; how they knew that what they planned and did would be appropriate.

To develop analytic understanding of subject teaching, research was needed, and Shulman was right that, in general, research on this aspect of teaching had been neglected. Largely as a result of his initiative, however, this has been less so in the past ten years. Brophy (1991), for example, was able to gather together and report the work of a considerable number of re-search projects on subject teaching.

Shulman's own concept of 'pedagogical content knowledge' has con-tinued to be the most influential way of thinking about the kind of teacher expertise involved in subject teaching. This knowledge

includes an understanding of what it means to teach a particular topic as well as knowledge of the principles and techniques required to do so. Framed by a conceptualization of subject matter for teaching, teachers hold knowledge about how to teach the subject, how learn-ers learn the subject (what are subject specific difficulties in learning, what are the developmental capabilities of students for acquiring particular concepts, what are common misconceptions), how curricu-lum materials are organized in the subject area, and how particular topics are best included in the curriculum. Influenced by both sub-ject matter and pedagogical knowledge, pedagogical content knowl-edge emerges and grows as teachers transform their content knowledge for the purposes of teaching.

(Wilson *et al.* 1987: 118)

At the core of pedagogical content knowledge is the idea that teachers transform their content knowledge for the purposes of teaching. At the centre, therefore, of pedagogical reasoning is this transformation process. This is said to involve four sub-processes: *critical interpretation* of the con-tent; consideration of alternative ways of *representing* the subject matter ('Ideally, teachers should possess a *representational repertoire* that consists of the metaphors, analogies, illustrations, activities, assignments and exam-ples that teachers use to transform the content for instruction'; Wilson *et al.* 119–20); *adaptation* of the teaching to take account of the characteristics of the student population; and *tailoring* the materials to the specific stu-dents in one class. The instruction that follows from this transformation process then leads on to evaluation, reflection and thence to a new en-riched comprehension.

If the above model is a valid representation of how subject teachers think in and for their teaching, then this provides us with a summary account of the craft of subject teaching we are seeking to understand. The extensive work of Shulman and his associates in recent years has certainly provided rich exemplification of the model, in particular with reference to the first two of the four transformation sub-processes. This work has also made three things increasingly clear. First, although their language and their examples often suggest a rather restricted range of teaching methods, with an emphasis on teacher exposition, their intention is that their model of pedagogical reasoning should encompass a wide range of teaching methods, including those which emphasize learning through activities. Second, however, there is a firm ideological commitment to the idea that pedagogical reasoning begins with comprehension of the con-tent and goes on to transformation of that content for teaching purposes. Third, and closely related, the model is clearly prescriptive as well as descriptive of good teaching; it is about what ideally should happen. There are clear echoes here, in the assumption that the necessary starting point for teaching is and should be the predetermined content to be taught, of the ideological debates associated with the National Curriculum in England.

Several researchers have meanwhile questioned, on empirical or con-ceptual grounds, the validity of this model, and indeed the helpfulness of 'pedagogical concept knowledge' as a concept. Marks (1990: 7), for exam-ple, found that the pedagogical reasoning of some of the mathematics teachers whom he studied involved the 'application of general pedagogical principles to particular subject matter contexts', rather than starting from the subject matter. Carter (1990: 306–7) suggests in relation to beginning teachers that 'it might well be that pedagogical content knowledge and classroom knowledge are not ultimately that different for learning teachers.' Pendry (1994) concludes from her review of relevant research that 'As yet we remain very ignorant about the extent to which, the ways in which and the circumstances in which pedagogy related to distinctive subject matter relates to the knowledge of other kinds that teachers use' (p. 214) and, from her own research on history student-teachers' learning, that 'as a way of understanding their conceptions of appropriateness, it seems the con-cepts of pedagogical content knowledge and reasoning do not do justice to the complexity and sophistication of the thinking of these novices' (p. 215).

Given our own concern to understand teachers' craft knowledge from their own perspectives, without importing our preconceptions, the work done on pedagogical content knowledge has perhaps been most helpful to us in alerting us to such preconceptions. The work of Shulman and his associates has been useful in opening up the field and in generating debate about the questions that need to be asked and assumptions that should be avoided. There have been other approaches to research on subject teaching developed in recent years, most notably the cognitive theory approach of Leinhardt (Leinhardt *et al.* 1991), though none so ambitious as Shulman's in the generality of their theorizing; and these too have been helpful in alerting us to questions to be asked and assumptions to be avoided. The nature of effective subject teaching, as understood, attempted and experienced by teachers and their pupils, is the central theme of this book.

## Taking account in the classroom of differences between pupils

Brown and McIntyre (1993) found that it was conditions relating to *pupils* that most commonly impinged upon teachers' choice of classroom action and upon the standards they used in evaluating the success of their teaching. Often these factors concerned the class as a whole, but more often it was characteristics of individual pupils or of sub-groups to which teachers referred, and it is on such differentiating characteristics that we decided to focus our attention in this study. In the context of their subject teaching, what differences among their pupils do teachers attend to, and in what ways do they take account of these differences?

A further distinction is made by Brown and McIntyre (1993) between two broad kinds of pupil characteristics to which teachers attended. The first type they exemplify by incidents in which teachers took account of pupils being 'shy', 'switched off', 'tired' and 'giggling'. And they add:

> Other teachers referred to pupils being fidgety, bored, hesitant, un-motivated, absent, excited, subdued, 'high', embarrassed, disruptive (as they arrive from another class), over-enthusiastic, bewildered, noisy, chattering, fussing, affected by other events outside the classroom and losing interest.
>
> (Brown and McIntyre 1993: 71)

They contrast such pupil conditions with the second type in the following way:

> In all the examples of pupil Conditions identified so far, the teachers have been *reacting* to some kind of 'sign', from individuals or the class as a whole, about their feelings, state of mind, physical well-being or cognition *on the day*. Although the teachers made frequent mention in this way of how pupils' immediate classroom behaviour imposed Conditions on their teaching, they referred more often to pupils' more enduring characteristics.
>
> (Brown and McIntyre 1993: 72)

They point out that when teachers know or perceive such enduring pupil characteristics, they can and sometimes do take account of them in a *proactive* way, not dependent on pupil behaviour on the day. They report that

> among the enduring individual pupil characteristics which teachers perceived as important, and as influencing the standards of NDS [normal desirable state] and Progress, were ability (general and specific), attention-seeking, self-confidence, lack of interest, motivation, tenacity, attentiveness, gender, maturity, attitudes, disruptive tendencies, laziness, poor grasp of English, noisiness and reticence. Some teachers clearly place most emphasis on what they see as permanent characteristics of their pupils, while others' accounts of their teaching attend much to pupils' behaviour on the day.
>
> (Brown and McIntyre 1993: 73)

Features of teachers' attention to differences among pupils that will interest us in this study include the kinds of differences to which teachers attend, and how teachers construe these differences, for example in terms of their stability.

Prominent among the pupil characteristics to which teachers attend, according to the research of Brown and McIntyre and many others, are differences in *ability*; and ability differences are always apparently construed by teachers as stable. How such ability differences should be understood, and how schools and individual teachers should deal with them, has been a consistently problematic and contentious issue, at both professional and political levels, for at least the past 50 years in the history of British schooling.

A simple way of dealing with stable differences in general academic ability or in specific subject abilities has often seemed to be by dividing pupils among a number of ability levels and teaching them in these relatively homogeneous groups. But

> the research on ability grouping shows that it often results in widening gaps in academic performance between high and low achievers, stigmatisation of lows, loss of self-esteem and motivation of lows, and restriction of friendship choices for cultural minorities . . . Teachers' expectations can be reflected in grouping decisions, and grouping often reinforces such expectations . . . The widening gap in performance between low and high groups, moreover, may result directly from instructional differences. Some research shows that, in addition to slower pacing with lower ability groups, teachers focus more on low-level objectives and routine procedures than they do with higher ability groups . . . In other words, there is a shift to different, or lower, instructional groups. Traditional ability grouping thus must be judged,

not maladaptive, if the goal is to maximise each student's opportunity to reach the same common goal . . . Furthermore, the teacher's task is *not* made uniform within ability groups, because students in such groups still differ in many other aptitudes for learning that are only moderately correlated, or even entirely uncorrelated with the measure used to form the groups.

(Corno and Snow 1986: 613)

It was on such very good grounds that in the 1960s and 1970s, along with the move towards comprehensive secondary schooling, there was a widespread shift in both primary and secondary schools to mixed ability teaching. It is necessary, however, to recognize that this organizational change alone has provided limited benefits. The findings of systematic research (e.g. Newbold 1977; Postlethwaite and Denton 1978; Slavin 1987, 1990) seem consistent with widespread experience in schools in indicating that mixed ability class grouping has substantial social benefits, but that in general it has no advantages or disadvantages in relation to educational attainments. Studies of teachers' experiences of mixed ability teaching (e.g. Reid *et al.* 1981) have reported that teachers frequently find classroom management more difficult in mixed ability classrooms and find it difficult to cater for all ability groups.

In recent years, British discussion of teaching in mixed ability classrooms has tended to focus on 'differentiation' according to pupils' abilities. Much of this discussion has lacked clarity about the purposes of differentiation; and in particular, British writers have generally not been clear about whether or not, in the words of Corno and Snow (1986), 'the goal [of differentiation] is to maximise each student's opportunity to reach the same common goal.' The complaint, however, stemming initially from Her Majesty's Inspectorate (1978), has been that teachers do not differentiate sufficiently in the tasks they set for pupils of different abilities; and more specifically that the tasks set are not well enough *matched* to these different abilities. This judgement has received strong support from research studies in primary schools in England (Bennett *et al.* 1984) and Scotland (Simpson 1989), both of which produced evidence that teachers, in the tasks they set, tended to overestimate the capabilities of children whom they saw as less able and even more to underestimate the capabilities of those they saw as more able.

Something of the complexity for teachers of taking account of differences in children's ability in the context of classroom teaching is revealed by Simpson, who reported her findings back to the participating teachers and sought their comments. The teachers agreed that the picture reported was probably a fair reflection of children's experience in their classrooms, and offered commentaries which may be briefly summarized as follows.

1 There were limits to the number of different groups of distinctive individuals with whom they could cope at any one time.
2 Having a wide spread of ability in their classes was greatly preferable in the interests of both teachers and children to grouping children into classes according to ability.
3 Whereas the study had been concerned only with pupils' 'academic' needs, it was also important to cater for their diverse social and emotional needs.
4 They deliberately gave special attention and extra resources to the lower ability groups, because their need for teaching help was greater.
5 More able children in the classroom were a valuable resource in that they offered models of effective learning and problem-solving that could help the learning of other children.
6 It was more useful for children's education to be broadened than for them to 'shoot ahead' of their peers; however, the provision of breadth depended on the availability of appropriate resources and of time.
7 While the research had concentrated on language tasks, it was also necessary to provide a wide curriculum.
8 If children appeared to be over-practising it was almost certainly related to the teachers' concern to ensure that the basic skills had been mastered; the teachers had to be mindful of prerequisites for the children's learning with the next teacher, the next stage of the curriculum or the next school to which they were going.

An important concern of this study will be to understand how such complex professional prioritization may inform and impose limitations upon the ways in which teachers take account of ability and other differences among their pupils.

It is not, however, inevitable that ability differences among pupils should be seen as necessarily stable and enduring. Bloom (1977), for example, has argued convincingly that an equally satisfactory way of describing and explaining ability differences among pupils is to see them as 'alterable variables', representing what pupils have or have not learned that they need for their further classroom learning. From such a perspective, noting of general ability and intelligence become superfluous, and the teacher's task becomes in large measure one of constantly ensuring that pupils have whatever understandings and skills he or she is going to depend on in teaching them. The educational attractions of this way of thinking are enormous, since it provides a framework for constructive thinking about every pupil's education. Yet the apparently less educationally constructive way of thinking – in terms of stable differences in general ability – has great practical advantages for teachers, in simplifying their task of making sense of differences among their pupils, and also perhaps in setting limits on what are seen as realistic targets for their pupils to attain. An important purpose of this research project is to seek an improved understanding of how the ways in which teachers construe the differences among their pupils are related both to their educational purposes and to the need to make their teaching task manageable.

Corno and Snow (1986) suggest that, whenever pupil 'aptitudes' are important for facilitating educational attainment, there are two possible strategies for helping pupils who are relatively lacking in these aptitudes: 'inaptitude circumvention' or 'aptitude development'. They point for example to the evidence on 'cooperative learning' (e.g. Slavin 1983; Webb 1983) as an example of inaptitude circumvention, whereby lower ability pupils are enabled to achieve higher levels of attainment as a result of working collaboratively in small groups with more able pupils. As an example of aptitude development, they cite the training of students in cognitive and metacognitive strategies (Weinstein and Mayer 1986). We shall be seeking to find out the inaptitude circumvention, aptitude development or other strategies that teachers use to help pupils whom they see to be lacking in important aptitudes.

In summary, then, our exploration of teachers' craft knowledge of taking account of differences between their students will be seeking answers to the following questions.

- Which differences among their pupils do teachers attend to?
- How do they construe these differences?
- How do their ways of construing differences relate to their educational purposes and their practical concerns?
- What considerations impinge on teachers' attention to and construal of differences and the ways they take account of them?
- What kinds of strategies do teachers adopt for taking account of differences?

## The craft knowledge of pupils as classroom learners

The primary *raison d'être* of schools and classrooms is that pupils should learn from them; and it follows that, although teachers are clearly crucial as facilitators, it is in terms of the success with which pupils engage in such learning that schools are largely judged. It is perhaps surprising, therefore, that relatively little attention has been given, at least until recently, to *how* pupils engage in classroom learning, or to the thinking and ideas that inform this engagement.

In Britain, the problem has not been that pupils' perspectives and classroom activities have been neglected by researchers. Especially at secondary school level there has been during the past 30 years a large number of studies concerned with pupils' activities in schools and classrooms, and with pupils' own ways of making sense of and responding to their situations. Among these studies are some of the best and most influential educational research investigations that have been conducted in this country. These studies are usefully synthesized by Woods (1990) under the title *The Happiest Days? How Pupils Cope with Schools*, which reflects very well the central themes of this strong British tradition: a focus on pupils' affective reactions to schooling, on their relationships with each other and with their teachers, and especially on pupils' own concerns and their strategies for pursuing these concerns.

Despite this emphasis on pupils' concerns and strategies, however, there is an almost total absence within this tradition of any mention of pupils' strategies for learning. This could be because pupils' approaches to school *work* have been the subject of relatively little study. It could be because research has focused primarily on relatively disaffected pupils, who have not presented themselves as being much concerned with school learning. On the other hand, it might be because pupils tend not to have strategies for learning but instead adopt passive approaches, either through lack of concern or because they see it as the teacher's responsibility to ensure that they learn.

Woods (1990), for example, while presenting learning as the primary concern of teachers ('Teachers would say their aim is to accomplish learning and that to learn, pupils have to work': p. 186), suggests both that 'Many pupils accept the need to be "made to work"' (p. 164) and that to succeed in maintaining good relations with pupils, teachers had to be

adept at humanizing the basic drudgery with departures from routine, attention to individuals, skilful use of laughter, converting 'work' to 'play' and so on. They will sell such activity to the pupils as 'play' both as a learning enterprise in itself and as a balance to more grisly business . . . Pupils might seek to transform any dull activity into play.
(Woods 1990: 175)

Woods then makes fairly explicit a message which is very strongly and clearly implicit in most of the research reports within this tradition: while pupils must be understood as creative strategists, drawing on diverse cultural resources, in their often oppositional ways of coping with school, there is no evidence of them bringing such strategic thinking to their classroom learning. In that respect pupils are at best prepared to let the teacher 'make them work', but in practice are more likely to force the teacher into compromising between the work needed for learning and pupils' other concerns. Do pupils not then develop any classroom craft knowledge which is conducive to their learning?

That seems unlikely: in that most pupils most of the time collaborate, enthusiastically or reluctantly, with their teachers in doing what the teachers see as classroom work, one might expect at least some of them to develop ways of setting about learning. To gain evidence of this, however, and to get some understanding of what it might involve, it seems necessary to turn to a very different tradition, a primarily North American one, of research into effective classroom teaching. By the 1980s, many researchers in this tradition had recognized that in order to understand the effects of classroom teaching upon pupils' achievements, they would need to study pupils' classroom thought processes.

Wittrock (1986: 297) begins his review of consequent research as follows:

> The recent research on student thought processes studies the effects of teachers and instruction upon the student perceptions, expectations, attentional processes, motivations, attributions, memories, generations, understandings, beliefs, attitudes, learning strategies and metacognitive processes that mediate achievement.

It is apparent that teachers are still seen as the major actors, with their effects on pupils' achievements being 'mediated' by their effects in the first instance on pupils' classroom thinking. Furthermore, if one looks particularly at research on pupils' learning strategies, one finds that the emphasis is very heavily on *teaching* pupils to use appropriate learning strategies (Weinstein and Mayer 1986; Wang and Palincsar 1989). None the less, research within this broad tradition has begun to tell us a good deal about the knowledge and expertise that pupils bring to their own classroom learning.

It is clear, for example, that as they get older and become more experienced in classrooms, pupils develop their strategies for learning. Thus research indicates that by the time they reach secondary school age pupils tend spontaneously

- to make more extensive use than younger children of such basic strategies as the use of rehearsal for memorizing information;
- to have developed capacities for using strategies that younger children seem to be unable to use, e.g. the production of their own imagery to relate to what they are seeking to learn and so to facilitate the learning;
- to use more sophisticated strategies for learning, e.g. organizing material for learning on the basis of its meanings rather than on more superficial bases.

Wittrock (1986) emphasizes especially the value for classroom learning of pupil strategies for generating relationships between what they are trying to learn and their own personal experiences and prior knowledge. He quotes impressive evidence about the effects upon achievement of pupils' adoption of strategies for, for example, relating stories read to them to their own life experiences, relating geographical ideas to concrete field trip experiences and actively linking events with principles to be learned.

Pupils appear to vary widely in the extent to which they believe they have control over the success of their own learning. Furthermore, as Coleman *et al.* (1966) and many other researchers since then have found, variation in this respect is highly related to the educational success that pupils go on to achieve. The extent to which pupils see the outcomes of their classroom activities, and of their schooling generally, as depending on their abilities, on their own efforts, on their choice of strategies, on the actions and judgements of their teachers or on other factors such as 'luck' is probably a very important influence both on their learning activities and on their achievements. Wang and Palincsar (1989: 76) summarize research findings in this area as follows:

> research suggests that the amount of effort that students are willing to put into a learning activity and their degree of persistence is determined by their expectations regarding success and failure, the value they give to the activity, and the extent to which they believe that their own strategic effort influences outcome . . . Students who believe that they control their learning are likely to use previously learned skills when acquiring new ones . . . An increase in a student's sense of personal control can lead, in turn, to greater self-responsibility, achievement motivation and learning.

The extent to which pupils are *aware* of their own learning strategies also seems to be related to the effectiveness of their learning. Peterson and Swing (1982), for example, found that, when other ability differences were controlled, the extent to which fifth and sixth grade pupils were able to describe the *specific* strategies they had used during lessons, but not global strategies such as 'thinking' or 'listening', was correlated with achievement.

Both pupils' knowledge about their learning processes and their control over these processes are elements of the important idea of *metacognition*, defined by Weinstein and Mayer (1986: 323) as 'students' knowledge about their own cognitive processes and their ability to control these processes by organizing, monitoring and modifying them as a function of learning outcomes.' The same authors report, for example, that pupils' understanding of material they have been trying to learn has consistently been shown to be related to the extent of their use of strategies for monitoring their own understanding of the material. Pupils need to know when they are not understanding; and they then need to be able to do something appropriate about it, perhaps something as apparently simple as asking for help.

One of our central concerns in this book is with the strategies that pupils use for learning in classrooms. While our concern is specifically with their strategies for learning, we shall not be presupposing that the strategies used by pupils are dependent on what teachers do, although that may well be the case. In this respect we see our project as being more similar to the British work synthesized by Woods (1990): our interest is in the pupils' own perspectives on their classroom learning activities, and we therefore adopt a more open approach than is used in most of the American research. Our simple premise, which is supported by the American work, is that just as teachers bring craft knowledge and expertise to their teaching, so pupils in secondary schools can be expected to bring craft knowledge and expertise to their classroom learning. We believe that it will be helpful to understand that knowledge and expertise better.

## Summary

In this chapter, we have sought to explain the research enterprise that this book reports, and the reasons for undertaking it. The general purpose is to extend previous work in the exploration of the professional knowledge and thought which teachers use in their day-to-day classroom teaching, their 'professional craft knowledge'. One of our aims, we have explained, is to test the generalizability of previous research findings about teachers' craft knowledge. Closely related to that is the intention to explore the impact, if any, of the National Curriculum context on teachers' craft knowledge and its use. Another aim is to look in a more focused way at particular aspects of the professional craft knowledge of teachers who are faced with what on the surface seems to be much the same task: thus the research is concentrated on teachers of English and teachers of history, teaching year 7 pupils in the context of the National Curriculum, and especially on their subject teaching and their ways of taking account of differences among pupils. Finally, we aim to explore the learning strategies of pupils in the same classrooms, an aspect of what may by analogy be seen as the pupils' classroom craft knowledge; and we shall seek to examine how, if at all, it relates to the professional craft knowledge of their teachers.

# 2 / Gaining access to teachers' and pupils' thinking: problems, principles and processes

In this chapter we offer an account of our research methods, and discuss some of the distinctive issues that it was necessary for us to address in putting our research plan into practice. The particular issues that concerned us are by no means unique to our study, but are likely to be encountered by other researchers seeking similar kinds of data. We therefore hope that this chapter will serve a dual purpose by providing:

1 An account of the particular methods which were used in our study, thus offering the reader an opportunity to evaluate the basis for the claims we make about our data.
2 A discussion of methodological issues of general interest to readers wishing to carry out similar studies.

## Building on antecedents of the current project

As has been shown in the previous chapter, the current study grew out of research carried out by Brown and McIntyre (1993). The first task of this chapter, therefore, is to show how research principles and procedures employed by Brown and McIntyre were utilized in the present study. It will then be shown that certain methodological adaptations and developments were required in an effort to achieve the distinctive objectives of the current study.

Brown and McIntyre's study set out to investigate successful classroom teaching, and the measures taken by teachers to achieve such success. The study was founded on the principle that any understanding of teaching will be severely limited unless it incorporates an understanding of how teachers themselves make sense of what they do: how they construe and evaluate their own teaching, how they make judgements, and why, in their own understanding, they choose to act in particular ways in specific circumstances to achieve their successes.

(Brown and McIntyre 1993: 1)

Brown and McIntyre also recognized that pupils' perceptions of classroom reality were an essential adjunct to teachers' perceptions, if they were to create a fully rounded picture of the lived reality of the classroom. They took four key measures intended to facilitate effective teacher and pupil engagement in the research process.

1 Emphasis on the positive. In their interviews with informants, Brown and McIntyre encouraged teachers and pupils to focus on aspects of teaching and learning that were successful. This measure was felt to motivate informants by removing possible anxieties that they might have about betraying trust, being unfairly critical of themselves and others. Furthermore, the technique reinforced the non-judgemental role of the researchers.
2 Focus on shared experiences. All interviews were preceded by a period of participant observation in lessons, so that the interviews could centre on experiences that the researchers and the informants had shared. This served a valuable purpose by enabling the researchers to validate informant claims about classroom occurrences. It also allowed the researchers to provide helpful prompts to informant recall.
3 Open approach in interviews. Brown and McIntyre adopted an 'open' approach in interviews by asking open-ended questions that focused on informants' individual perspectives. This measure ensured that informants' accounts were not pre-formed by researcher bias.
4 Overtly helping teachers and pupils to access the required information. Brown and McIntyre took particular steps to minimize the potentially negative effects of the necessary delay that took place between observed lessons and in-depth interviews. They interviewed pupils as soon after lessons as was convenient, while they interviewed teachers for approximately two minutes at the end of each lesson. The contents of this brief teacher interview were then used to stimulate recall in the final longer interviews.

Methodological antecedents of the present study can also be located in research carried out by one of the present authors into teachers' and pupils' perceptions of residential schooling for pupils with emotional and behavioural difficulties (Cooper 1989, 1993a,b,c). This study set out to identify teachers' and pupils' perceptions of the schools where they worked or were resident, in an effort to gain insight into the effects of the schools on pupil outcomes. As in the case of Brown and McIntyre's research, this was an exploratory study, which required the researcher to create circumstances that would enable staff and pupils to express their personal views, rather than to respond to predetermined questions generated by the researcher. Here it was found, in the course of the pilot study, that the quality of the interview data was enhanced when the interviewer consciously employed measures during interviews that were derived from the work of the humanistic psychologist Carl Rogers (1951, 1980). Furthermore, it was found that when these measures were employed in the researcher's informal interactions with participants that ease of interaction was facilitated. These measures are summarized below.

*Empathy.* The interviewer showed informants that he was willing and able to empathize with their expressed views, however idiosyncratic these might be. This often involved responding to informant statements, or prefacing requests for elaboration with a statement something like: 'I find it very understandable that you see the situation you have described in the way you do. I'm sure, given what you've said about x, if I had had that experience, I would have responded as you did.' This was felt to be a necessary measure to enable informants to express their personally held views, by showing that their views were both understood and accepted.

*Unconditional positive regard.* The interviewer showed an overt sense of liking and interest in informants as individuals, through verbal (e.g. use of preferred name, humour, enquiries into personal well-being) and non-verbal cues (e.g. forward posture, maintenance of eye contact). This helped to give informants a sense of comfort and security, and was calculated to minimize defensive responses.

*Congruence.* The interviewer strove as far as possible to ensure that his input into the interview dialogue would be perceived by the informant as honest and authentic. This involved, for example, asking for clarification of contradictions and inconsistencies in informant statements, and requiring informants to relate generalized statements to specific incidents that, where possible, had been observed by the interviewer. This helps to motivate informants to present authentic responses.

*Repeat probing.* This technique is not Rogerian in origin. The present authors use the term to describe the process whereby, during interviews or informal talk, informants are unable to respond effectively to a request for elaboration, clarification or exemplification. Where this happens, the researcher overtly accepts this situation, but repeats the request later in the interview as and when the opportunity arises. Experience has shown that this technique often succeeds in helping the interviewee to access information, while avoiding the use of heavy handed prompting.

The combination of these antecedents provided a firm basis on which to develop the research project that is the subject of this book. In the following sections it will be shown precisely how we employed the fruits of this experience, and how we addressed those distinctive aspects of the current research task that took us beyond our previous experience.

## Background features of the current study

The present study is based on the idea that experienced teachers and pupils are in possession of extensive and complex 'craft knowledge' that enables them to engage in effective teaching and learning in classrooms, at least some of the time. The theory of craft knowledge that underpins the project is derived from work by Desforges and McNamara (1977, 1979) and Brown and McIntyre (1993). The criteria for what is meant by 'effective' are part of teachers' and pupils' craft knowledge, as is the knowledge of means by which such effectiveness is achieved. The intention of the research is to access and describe this knowledge, and to explore the ways in which teachers' and pupils' perceptions can be related one to the other. In addition to the concern with craft knowledge, the research seeks access to the related areas of teachers' ways of construing and taking account of individual differences among pupils, and teachers' responses to the newly introduced National Curriculum (to England and Wales) in English and history.

The experience of the Brown and McIntyre study sensitized us to some of the difficulties that may be involved in the processes of retrieving and articulating this knowledge. We cannot assume, for example, that ideas about effective teaching and learning are foremost in the thinking of teachers and pupils in the aftermath of lessons (Brown and McIntyre 1993). However, while the previous study was almost entirely exploratory, the specific questions of the current study, relating to subject knowledge, catering for differences and the National Curriculum, meant that we were faced with a greater tension between our own agenda as researchers and the agenda of the pupils and teachers in our study. Our task was to develop methods that would facilitate the articulation of teachers' and pupils' authentic concerns about these matters, without constraining the scope or content of these concerns. The prescriptive, theory-based dimension of the study, therefore, introduced a distinctive tension that had to be acknowledged and dealt with in our research design and procedures.

### Participants

Eight English teachers, five history teachers and one year 7 (pupils aged 11–12 years) class per teacher participated in this study. A total of 325 pupils were in the classes studied, of whom 288 were interviewed. The English teachers represented two from each of four different schools, while three schools were represented among the history teachers: two teachers from each of two schools, and one from a third school. All of the participants were from local education authority comprehensive schools. The main criteria employed when we were identifying potential participating departments was the likelihood that they would contain a sufficient number of staff who were: interested and willing to participate in a study of this kind; in at least their third year of teaching. It was also necessary that the senior management of the schools was likely to be supportive of research of this kind.

Additionally, the schools had to be within a reasonable travelling radius of the university. Difficulties experienced in recruiting history departments led to this radius extending to 50 miles for one department, though the remainder were located between 10 and 30 miles from the university. Schools from three different LEAs were used.

*Procedures*

The aim of the research was to enable teachers and pupils to articulate their understandings of effective classroom teaching and learning. The chief method chosen to achieve this was informant style interviewing (Powney and Watts 1987). The researcher engaged in participant observation during lessons and conducted separate interviews with teachers and a sample of pupils after each lesson. In order to see the lessons in the context of an ongoing process of teaching and learning, the study focused on sequences of lessons which made up curriculum units. A 'unit' is defined as a consecutive series of lessons, involving approximately four (or in some cases six) hours work, and considered by the teacher to be to some degree self-contained in terms of their collective coherence from a teaching viewpoint. Furthermore, in order to understand how different content and also developing teacher–pupil relationships might influence patterns of teaching and learning, where possible two or three such units were studied for each teacher and class, at different times of the year. In all, 32 such units of teaching and learning were studied, with eight of the 13 teachers and their classes being followed by three separate units spread over the academic year. The remaining five teachers were studied for a single six-hour unit each.

*Sampling pupils*

At the outset of the project it was intended that all the pupils in all the classes studied would be interviewed. This aspiration, however, proved impractical in certain cases, owing to time restrictions and clashes between interview times and pupils' extra-curricular commitments. In order to minimize the potentially negative effects of failing to interview all pupils a sampling procedure was operated. This involved gathering data from the teachers about their perceptions of individual differences among members of the teaching group, through interviews and brief written comments. On the basis of these data it was possible to ensure that the pupils interviewed were broadly representative in terms of the salient differences among them as perceived by teachers.

*Group, pair and individual interviews*

All the teachers were interviewed individually. With pupils, however, it was decided to employ group, pair and individual interviews. There were a number of reasons for this.

The first factor was *pupil comfort and motivation*. We were conscious from the outset that the kind of involvement that our research required would be a new experience for many of the pupils in our study. Added to this was the fact that these were 11–12-year-old pupils who were embarking on their first year of secondary schooling, and for some of them the interviews were to take place only four or five weeks into their first term. We were aware that the combination of these circumstances might appear daunting and a source of potential discomfort to all but the most confident of pupils. It was therefore decided, in the initial encounters with year 7 pupils, to interview them in groups of between three and five. This enabled us to invite a range of pupils to interview, rather than simply relying on the most confident. The interviews were made deliberately informal. It was found that once one or two such interviews had been conducted a rapport was established with at least some of those who had participated, and this helped to promote a positive public image of the research to other pupils. After one or two such interviews, therefore, it became easier to elicit the cooperation of individuals and pairs of pupils in interviews.

The second factor was *group processes and individual thinking*. Our initial intention was to explore pupils' individual thinking about their classroom experiences, and this remained a central theme of the research. However, in the course of early group interviews we discovered unexpected opportunities to gain insight into group processes and the effects of collaborative working on pupil learning. This was particularly the case where groups and pairs of interviewees had been working collaboratively during the observed lesson. By and large, however, pupils were interviewed individually, the particular value of the inividual interview being that it creates the opportunity for pupils to explore their recollections and thinking in depth. The group interview inevitably produces a group response, which, as we have suggested, can be valuable for certain purposes.

The third factor was *individual preferences*. While, once the research was underway in each school, the vast majority of pupils were willing, and in some cases eager, to be interviewed on an individual basis, some pupils remained reticent and expressed a preference for being interviewed with one or two friends. In the interests of pupil motivation the researcher accepted this situation. Where appropriate the pupil in question was urged to choose a person or people with whom he or she had been working. In the event the researcher usually made the invited pupil's thinking the focus of the interview.

The final pragmatic reason for employing group interviews was to ensure a high degree of *coverage* of the pupil population.

## The methodological task

The methodological task set out for us by our research questions can be defined in terms of two questions that are of perennial concern to qualitative researchers. Both questions relate to the problematic relationship that we felt would necessarily exist between us as researchers and the teachers and pupils who were being researched. Our chief concern was with the fine line between, on the one hand, allowing the teachers and pupils to be expansive and, on the other, seeking answers to our research questions. The key challenges here were as follows.

- How could we successfully motivate teachers and pupils to put the necessary time and effort into revealing their authentic thoughts and concerns about the specific issues that were of concern to us?
- How could we deal with the possibility that the teachers and pupils might present merely plausible as opposed to authentic responses to our requests for information?

Both of these questions will now be dealt with in greater detail, along with some of the answers we generated.

Of central importance in research of any kind is the need to achieve an appropriate fit between the research objectives and the research method. In the present case, because the research objectives demanded considerable personal effort and involvement by the teachers and pupils, particular attention was paid to the kind of relationships that the researcher developed with the teachers and pupils.

### Motivating teachers and pupils

Our first step in this process was to identify the demands that the research would make on teachers and pupils.

First of all, we wanted our informants to share with us their authentic understanding of what in practice they took to be good teaching and learning in the classrooms we were studying and of factors they experienced as having an influence on the quality of teaching and learning in the classrooms we are studying. Second, we acknowledged the demands that our intentions would place on our informants. We had to recognize that while sense-making processes are central to teachers' and pupils' normal activities, the articulation of these processes is far more important to the researcher than to the teacher or pupil. Furthermore, this articulation process is both demanding, owing to its difficulty, and potentially threatening to those concerned with possible perceived weaknesses in their thinking or practice.

In order to facilitate motivation we presented the project, from the outset, as being based on the idea that experienced teachers and pupils are in possession of extensive and complex knowledge that enables them to engage in effective teaching and learning. The criteria for 'effectiveness' and the meaning of the term 'learning' are themselves part of this knowledge, as is the means by which these are achieved. The researcher's role, therefore, was to stimulate teachers and pupils to recall and describe this knowledge. We felt it important to emphasize that the researcher's role was quite distinct from those of the teacher and pupil and did not place him in a position to judge teacher or pupil. In this sense the teacher and the pupils were cast as the unrivalled 'experts' in their own fields.

The accessing procedure played an important role in establishing appropriate relationships. Before formal approaches were made to headteachers, the heads of departments in selected schools were approached on an informal basis, with information about the project. Only if members of the department declared a willingness to commit sufficient time to the project were the headteachers of schools approached with a formal request to carry out the research.

Pupils present a slightly different set of problems from teachers, in that initial approaches to them are nearly always made via the teachers. This unfortunate necessity carries with it the hidden danger that the researcher may become too closely associated in the minds of pupils with the authority structures of the school (see Ball 1985). This is a distinctive problem when one is seeking an understanding of pupils' effective classroom learning. When one's primary concern is with pupils' social relationships or with their (often negative) reaction to schooling, it is relatively easy to communicate one's interest in their own unofficial agendas. It is much more difficult to distance oneself from a teacher perspective, and to persuade pupils that one is interested in their distinctive expertise – not their perceptions of official right answers – when one's concern is with effective classroom learning strategies. Furthermore, when one's concern *is* with classroom learning it is all the more necessary that one's access to the pupils is through their classroom teacher.

In order to overcome this problem the fieldworker took a number of measures designed to give pupils a sense of control over their involvement in the project. Before engaging in observation work with the pupils, the researcher spent time mixing in a fairly informal way with pupils in lessons. Only once a degree of rapport had been established did the researcher invite pupils for interview. When a pupil was invited to interview, the voluntary nature of his or her participation was stressed by allowing the pupil to select a day and time that was suitable to him or her (this necessarily involves breaktimes or lunchtimes). The researcher actively avoided giving the impression that he was able to arrange for interviews in lesson time, as this might have encouraged pupils to view the researcher as an authority figure with an official status within the school. For similar reasons the researcher stressed the confidentiality of pupil interview data.

While the researcher was aware of the need to avoid presenting himself as an authority figure to both teachers and pupils, he was also careful to avoid behaving in a way that would upset the expectations that teachers and pupils have about appropriate adult behaviour. The researcher was not a member of staff, and neither was he a pupil. The researcher had to combine approachability and trustworthiness with the image of being of a status worthy of teachers' and pupils' time and effort. So although the researcher did not wish to be identified, in the eyes of pupils, directly with the authority structure of the school, it was also important to remember that the pupils would be likely to share certain expectations regarding the conduct of relations between adults and children. Adults are, by and large, expected by children to be, if not authority figures, at least authoritative. Thus, for the researcher to have refused to help the pupils with their schoolwork when they approached him, for example, might well have undermined the pupils' view of the researcher as a person to be trusted and respected. Similarly, in dealing with teachers, it was felt to be important that the researcher should present himself as alert and informed in relation to the current state of English education and schools, while at the same time being someone who needed the intricacies of teaching in their specific contexts explained to him. In short, the researcher strove to combine ease of manner, trustworthiness and approachability with the presentation of an image of being of a status worthy of the informants' time and effort. Only when this is achieved can the researcher expect to be given the necessary access to less superficial levels of experience.

Some of the key points so far covered relating to subject motivation will now be illustrated with examples from interview data gathered in the pilot study.

*Informant as expert*

In order to manage effectively the tension that we experienced between the conflicting needs (a) to answer specific research questions and (b) to allow the informants to be open and expansive it was necessary to pay considerable attention to the ways in which we elicited responses in interviews. The essential thing here, we decided, was to strive for a collaborative relationship between researcher and respondent, with the identification of a common agenda, as well as its exploration, being an ongoing task. The aim was to give the respondent the experience of engaging in a conversation with the researcher which was directed by a commonality of interest, rather than by either the researcher's questions alone or the informant's current concerns alone.

By overtly emphasizing the teacher's expertise and showing an awareness of the difficulties involved in articulating craft knowledge, we established a collaborative relationship between teachers and researcher, in which they together explored the teacher's thinking. An example of this type of collaboration is provided below. The example demonstrates the way in which researcher and informant help to refine one another's thinking, in order to get a clear impression of what the informant is recalling. The interviewer is here addressing a research question relating to the teacher's ways of dealing with individual differences, but doing this in such a way as to emphasize the relationship between the question and the teacher's already stated personal concerns. The question, therefore, takes on the guise of a request for elaboration, rather than a straightforward question derived from the researcher's agenda. In this example the teacher has been describing the beginning phase of a lesson, in which he has recapped on the previous lesson (I is interviewer):

*I:*  I was thinking about the bit at the beginning of the lesson: the questioning. You were saying [earlier in the interview] that you weren't very happy. How did you select those pupils then, who you asked [to answer questions]? What was your thinking behind that?

*Mr Turtle:*  I was looking for a sort of benchmark, erm . . . towards the end, but not right off the bottom. I know, if they got it, then most of the rest of the class have anyway. Without picking on James Spear who has tremendous difficulty remembering . . . Er, and Tim Mablethorpe. Although I did end up talking to Ja – the one on the far left at the end, who was having difficulties. But I mean partly too, you also hope that, if these people get it right – tremendous kudos for them, and tremendous feeling of self-esteem in having grown. If they get it wrong, it backfires on you. But yes, I was simply – I was looking for the weaker members of the class; the ones who do not have a great retentive memory; who don't always pay attention as much as they should. And to see what they had got out of it; what they had remembered . . .

*I:*  Did you feel then, that you got to a point in that introductory phase, where you were satisfied that they had it?

*Mr Turtle:* Yes. Yes.

*I:*       How did –

*Mr Turtle:* No. No, sorry. Not satisfied that they had it. Satisfied that we had had sufficient exposure in the classroom, to reactivate some memories. To be thinking again of these terms. I don't think they'll have it, Paul, until . . . Some of them have got it already, quite obviously; some of them won't have it until – perhaps not even by – the end of their schooling. I don't know perhaps they'll still be making confusions.

   This extract illustrates the way in which the collaborative approach produces a refined response which is rooted in the teacher's understandings. The teacher's answer to the first question, with its references to his own actions and his interactions with particular pupils, shows that his account is grounded in actual classroom events. With the second question the researcher has introduced the term 'had it', based on the teacher's use of the term 'got it', meaning 'absorbed the required knowledge'. Having been introduced to the term, the teacher appears to juggle with it, at first rejecting it as a description of the criterion he was using at that point in the lesson; then examining the appropriateness of the term. He finally concludes that the term may apply to the learning of some pupils, but not all. At the same time the teacher rejects 'had it', and replaces it with 'exposure'. Another example is provided in an interview with a history teacher.

*I:*       What about when you did ask questions, and you selected, very carefully, it seemed to me, the pupils who answered the questions. Did you, or was that my perception?

*Mr Cole:* No. I was trying to do –. I was trying to think in terms . . . subconsciously, of a balance between boys and girls; also between able and not so able. So I was trying to spread it out, y'know . . .

*I:*       I wondered if, for instance, if you were choosing particular pupils to answer particular questions.

*Mr Cole:* No, no. There was no kind of policy in it.

Here the teacher refines the researcher's perception of the teacher's questioning strategy. In fact he is saying that he did choose his respondents carefully, but by a different criterion from that suggested by the researcher. These extracts also demonstrate each subject's determination to produce his own account and an unwillingness to be led meekly by the researcher's definitions.

   In the following sections it will be shown that this 'collaborative' approach manifests itself in many different ways in the researcher–informant relationships that we established.

*Researcher knowledge and informant motivation*

The other side of the 'informant as expert' coin, with its implications for
the relative status of researcher and subject, is the question of researcher
credibility. As has already been noted, the researcher must avoid dominat-
ing the informants while maintaining a persona that complies with subjects'
notions of acceptability (see Hammersley and Atkinson 1983). However,
a central problem in the present research was related to the potential
difficulties involved in developing a persona that was acceptable to both
pupils and their teachers. As Ball (1985) observes, this is a not uncommon
problem for researchers in schools.

As it transpired, a particular strength of the present research approach
lies in the fact that the researcher is participating in two communities of
informants. The wide differences in status and function between these two
communities mean that the researcher's involvement with both gives him
access to a greater breadth of knowledge than that which is held by
members of either community. The researcher's presence in the classrooms,
and the fact that he made audio recordings of classroom events, provided
an important signal to both teachers and pupils that the researcher was
well informed as to the pattern of events taking place during the unit
lessons. Moreover, since the researcher conducted the majority of his in-
lesson interactions with pupils, and spent a considerable amount of time
interviewing pupils outside of lessons, the teachers became aware that the
researcher's knowledge of the pupil perspective on the lessons was far
more detailed than their own:

> I was trying to think in terms of a balance . . . between boys and girls;
> also between able and not so able. So I was trying to spread it out,
> y'know. And I don't know if I missed anyone out . . . I dunno. [to
> researcher] Did I miss anyone out?
>
> (Mr Cole)

> Can't remember what I said at the end of the last lesson. [laughs]
> What did I say? What did I say?
>
> (Mr Turtle)

> And then you got the group – 'People' [group] – not the people
> group! Which one's Jim in?
>
> (Ms Pitt)

> You've interviewed him [a pupil], so you know more than I do about
> what he sees as being his purpose.
>
> (Ms Pitt)

I would consider Liz to be relatively weak in terms of this type of skill. She was one of the ones you interviewed, so it would be interesting to see what she got out of it.

(Mr Cole)

The indication here is that the researcher is seen by the teachers as a well informed observer who is not solely dependent on the teachers for information. The possibility that the researcher might be able to offer the teacher some insight into aspects of classroom life which are normally outside of the teacher's field of awareness is also a source of motivation to teachers. Furthermore, the fact that the teacher is not privy to some of the researcher's knowledge (particularly that pertaining to pupils) helps to minimize the temptations for teachers to invent plausible answers rather than to try to recall and to clarify their reasons for acting as they did. It would also seem to be the case that any motivation to deceive the researcher is weakened by the focus of the interview questions, which concentrate deliberately on the teachers' perceptions of what they have done well in the lessons studied, and thus avoid the use of questions that might appear to threaten to undermine the teachers' professional competence.

For pupils, the novelty of being a research informant was a motivating factor (a point also noted by Ball 1985). The fact that the researcher showed an interest in pupil opinions was clearly flattering to many pupils. This was demonstrated in pupils' enthusiasm and willingness to participate in the study. On the other hand, because of the researcher's inevitable associations with 'the adult "team"' (Ball 1985), coupled with the researcher's efforts to fulfil their expectations of him as a respectable adult, the pupils readily cooperated in the research enterprise. As with the staff, the researcher's participation in the events that were the focus of interviews added to pupils' confidence in the fact that the researcher was knowledgeable and well informed. This was demonstrated in the current study by the fact that pupils often asked the researcher to verify the accuracy of their recall of events in lessons.

*Motivating informants to give authentic as opposed to plausible answers*

The present study is principally concerned with the thinking that underlies teachers' and pupils' classroom activity. It was necessary, therefore, to devise a strategy to enable the researcher and informant to distinguish between responses which represent such thinking, and responses which are *post hoc* rationalizations of behaviour with little or no relationship to informants' usual patterns of interactive thinking, or expressions of espoused rather than practised theory.

*Interview rationale*

In order to deal with this problem a method of 'informant' style (Powney and Watts 1987) interviewing was adopted. The rationale of informant interviews is that the interviewer allows the shape and direction of the interview to be largely dictated by the unfolding pattern of the interviewee's perspective. In the present study the interview method is designed to facilitate the interviewees' recall of particular and personal cognitive representations of the lessons being studied. This approach draws on models of storage and recall of memory traces, which stress the importance of associative dimensions of traces (Baddeley 1990). Put simply, this suggests a model of human memory as a network of interconnected memory traces, some of which are more readily available to recall than others. The recall of less readily available traces is facilitated by following the lines of connection between the more available and less available traces. The lines of connection themselves are individual and idiosyncratic. The approach bears interesting associations with the technique of 'cognitive interviewing' (Roy 1991), in its adherence to the view that accurate recall can often depend on the pursuit of idiosyncratic connections, involving the activation of cues that may have no obvious relevance to anyone other than the informant. Informants are initially encouraged to recall any aspect of the lesson that is prominent in their memories. These 'surface features' are then explored and developed through a process of elaboration, which is based on the researcher's use of prompts. The intention of this approach is to ensure that interviewees' accounts are grounded in their perceptions of the actual events of lessons. Where interviewees do make generalized remarks the researcher requests exemplification. It is, therefore, possible to distinguish between responses that are so grounded and those that are not. Similarly, responses relating to events that have been directly observed and recalled by the researcher can be considered to have a higher degree of reliability than those that relate to events not observed by the researcher.

In the final analysis it is those items of interview data which are most thoroughly grounded in classroom events, and expounded with consistency and intricate detail, that form our most useful and interesting data.

One of the valuable things about this approach is that it frees informants to explore their own concerns, within the limits of the research categories, and, therefore, facilitates subject confidence from the outset. This applies to both teachers and pupils. The following examples illustrate the way in which most of the pupil interviews began, with the researcher asking an open-ended question and the informants offering confident and content-rich replies:

*I:*    What was that lesson about, that you've just been in?
*Zoe:*  Erm, well, you were learning about verbs, but you had a story board. You had to make up a story . . . in our groups. And everyone had to

put verbs and things in it, and make it quite specific, and write a paragraph about it.

*I:*  What were you learning about in English today?

*Sam:*  Well, in English today . . . Last week, in our reports, we all wrote what we really felt. And some of us had a bit of trouble working in groups and cooperating. And the idea of today's lesson was to help you overcome those and cooperate with everybody else.

*I:*  What were you learning about in that lesson?

*Pat:*  Sort of to cooperate with each other, and take it in turns to . . . and . . . sort of to use our imagination and things, and sort of think of what an island would be like. And then we had to do the name, and . . . using our imagination, and erm, drawing something on it.

On the few occasions where pupils were unable to answer this initial question, or provided confused answers, the researcher guided the informant to a specific area of consideration:

*I:*  What were you learning about in that lesson?

*Lyn:*  Erm. Don't know really. [laughs]

*I:*  OK. What did you actually do in today's lesson, then?

*Lyn:*  Sort of done some more planning towards our film. Put it all together. And erm . . . got it ready for showing to the rest of the class.

*I:*  What were you learning about in that lesson with Mr X?

*Ron:*  Erm . . . er, how to, er . . . put words to pictures, that you didn't understand what they really were . . .

*I:*  OK. So, 'how to put words into pictures'. I know I was there, and I saw what was happening, but can you imagine that I wasn't there. Exactly what were you doing?

*Ron:*  Erm, editing pictures . . .

*I:*  Right.

*Ron:*  . . . into words.

In each of these cases the researcher guides the pupil to reflect on her or his experience in the lesson, and thus signals that the interview is to be grounded in this area of personal recollection.

As the interview develops, the researcher attempts to guide the informant towards more detailed accounts of the cognitions underlying the lesson or unit concerned. This second level of questioning may be, for the informant, of a higher magnitude of difficulty, in the sense that he or she is being asked to recall aspects of the situation that may or may not have been consciously considered at the time. The approach bears some similarity with that described by Logan (1984), particularly in relation to his idea of 'levels of discourse'. Unlike Logan, however, we are not claiming access to the 'authentic self' of the informant, as much as to the informant's authentic perceptions of matters which are of interest to us. It is appropriate to see these interviews as exploring various strands in the complex web of informants' recall of thoughts and events. We can accept Logan's notion of 'levels' or 'layers', if we consider these terms as referring to researcher-generated categories. In this sense the 'superficial' layers are of peripheral interest to the researcher, while the 'deep' or 'high' level responses are those that are of interest. The identification of a chosen 'surface feature' provides a starting point from which a web of associations is traced. The researcher's task is to motivate the subject to trace strands that yield elaboration and exemplification of interesting areas.

In the present study the value of this approach is supported by the ways in which informants' (both pupils' and teachers') recall of external events and internal states is clearly facilitated by their receiving opportunities to approach questions from different perspectives, starting from their idiosyncratic recall of situations (see Roy 1991). It is suggested that the idiosyncratic information provides important contextual cues that enable the informant to gain access to more salient information. In the following extract an unpromising opening sequence develops into a rich account of the boy's internal thought processes and how these are influenced by the teacher's behaviour. It is important to note that this penetration is achieved not through the use of heavy handed prompting, but through a careful probing of the emerging picture of the lesson presented by the pupil. The opening exchange of the interview is typical of the study as a whole:

*I:* What do you remember the lesson was about?
*Tim:* Ms Pitt told us about what we were supposed to be doing, and we had to write a small essay about how we got on to the island . . . We had to draw the island, bit by bit; each person drew a little bit . . .

The pupil stops, at first for an apparent pause, but does not continue, so the interviewer intervenes:

*I:* Yes, well . . . Is that it? Or is there any more to it?
*Tim:* I can't think of anything else.

This faltering beginning suggests that the boy's recall of the lesson is vague. The researcher perseveres, however, accepting the pupil's account of the lesson, and moving on to the second broad category of investigation:

*I:* Right. Now, what things happened in the lesson that really helped you to learn about those things?

A long pause is brought to a close when the researcher rephrases the question:

*I:* Was there anything that you felt helpful in the lesson in getting you to learn?

*Tim:* Writing the essay helped. So we knew what we were doing; it helped us to understand what the whole thing was about.

The obvious 'English' content here seems to be the essay writing exercise; the pupil's remarks, however, do not seem to be leading towards any explanation of how the essay writing was facilitated. At this stage, therefore, the interview is looking unpromising. The researcher continues, however, to accept the pupil's definition of the situation, and simply seeks further elaboration:

*I:* How did that help you then: the actual writing of the essay?

*Tim:* When I was writing, it made me think more about what we were doing, and what's happening on the island and what it's like.

The researcher then moves on to a third category of interest, namely the role of other people in the learning process:

*I:* Was there anything that Ms Pitt did that was particularly helpful to you?

*Tim:* . . . Apart from she came round and helped us with part of the essays.

*I:* How did she help you?

*Tim:* She helped us with spellings. She helped us with what to say and what words to put. Instead of putting short sentences; put with more expression.

*I:* How did she do that then? Did she just tell you to do that or . . .

*Tim:* No, she told us to think of more . . . words that explain things better.

*I:* Can you think of an example of her doing that?

*Tim:* Er . . . I put: 'I got hit by a plane, coming from behind.' And she told me to put something like: 'I was flying low and I got shot at from behind. It hit me in the wing.'

So far, these extracts indicate the way in which the pupil's recall of the lesson becomes increasingly personalized. His cursory account of the lesson content at the beginning of the interview develops into a quite detailed account of specific events, and eventually develops into an account of cognitive process:

*I:* Did she [the teacher] actually tell you to put those words?

*Tim:* Well, she helped me think of them.

*I:* Can you remember how she did that?

*Tim:* She just . . . Dunno! . . . She just told me to think of some better words, that would sound better in the story.

*I:* Is that what she said? She said, 'think of some words that will sound better in the story.'

*Tim:* She said – well, I don't know what she actually said. She said, 'think of some words that will sound better in the story.'

*I:* . . . Did you think it was better, what you wrote the second time?

*Tim:* Yes.

*I:* What happened then? Can you remember what you were thinking, when you did that?

*Tim:* I was just thinking what it would really be like, and what to put. I was thinking of words to put down.

*I:* So you were thinking of what it would really be like to be flying an aeroplane and being shot at. What were you thinking about when you first of all wrote down: 'I was flying in a plane and I was hit,' or whatever it was you wrote the first time?

*Tim:* Yes.

*I:* What were you thinking about then . . . Do you remember what you were thinking about then?

*Tim:* I don't think I was thinking about the story, I was thinking about other things, not the story. I was writing anything that fitted.

Here the pupil is recalling the process by which the teacher's intervention focused his attention on the work in hand, and encouraged him to engage in imaginative construction of the event he was attempting to portray. Furthermore, the pupil recalls his own sense of having improved on the original draft.

The teacher interviews followed a similar pattern, and this can be illustrated with reference to the same incident that was described by the pupil above. In this example we can observe the way in which the teacher's recall is enhanced when she thinks aloud, beginning with superficial – apparently irrelevant – cues. She has been talking about the way in which she 'circulates' around the class when the pupils are engaged in written work, in order to monitor progress and give individual help. The researcher has asked her whether she remembers helping Tim:

*I:* Right. So is it difficult for you to remember what you might have been thinking, when you stopped at Tim?

*Ms Pitt:* I think he did come up to me actually. I think I remember standing in the middle of the room with his book, and thinking, first of all – the first thing I thought about was his writing, cos he was trying out lots of different writing styles: they're always different. I remember thinking it was better. I do remember that. Cos it was bigger.

*I:* Bigger?

*Ms Pitt:* Bigger writing. He was writing very, very, very tiny . . . I remember the initial look of it, and then reading it through, and then – it was all that side about the aeroplane, and that much [indicating

a small amount] on the island. That's the first thing I pointed out
to him. Yes, he came up to me and said, 'miss', sort of thing . . . Cos
he's very – he's demanding, Tim. He's been picked up in other
lessons. He won't wait; he won't put his hand up. He'll just come
and get you, and speak to you, even if you are talking to somebody else.

I:           What were you interested in then, when you were looking at his
             work?

Ms Pitt:  Erm, I wasn't looking at spellings or punctuation. I was looking
             at his ideas, and what his perception of the island was. Cos at that
             point all they'd done was draw the map; they hadn't actually gone
             off into their groups and started on what they wanted to be there.
             So I wanted to see if they were coming up with a consensus of
             how it was going to be, or whether it was very different.

I:           So what would have been your reaction if it had been OK in that
             way?

Ms Pitt:  I'd have praised him. I'd probably still – cos if he'd finished that
             quick, I doubt if he'd have developed it to the full – to his full
             ability. And I'd have probably asked for a bit more detail, and
             said, 'maybe you could walk a little further through the jungle' . . .
             He in fact, I remember thinking – I do remember now thinking
             it was very urban; using shops and streets, and cars and things.
             Where most of the others had slightly more – they were on a
             beach, or . . .

This shows the way in which the teacher reconstructs the situation under
discussion by recalling three key mnemonics. The first is the size of Tim's
handwriting; the second relates to the broad intentions she had (to establish pupils' 'perceptions of the island'); the third involves reconstructing the logic behind her intervention with Tim ('if he'd have finished that
quick I doubt if he'd have developed it to the full'). While much of this
detail may appear irrelevant to the question of how the teacher approached
the task of helping Tim with his written work, all these details are points
of reference for the teacher, and they enable her to reconstruct the situation mentally. Each newly constructed piece in the cognitive jigsaw provides
cues to indicate how to develop the existing picture:

His book's come back to me now, and I'm picturing it. I remember,
that his first piece was quite short. And then he – I remember taking
– I think it was his work – I took it all in, to look at the homework.
And I think his second draft – he'd actually started again, and written
again, and it was longer . . . I was aware that he hadn't taken time
thinking about the first draft. This is why I spent some time asking
him to explain what he was doing.

Finally, the teacher has reached a point where she can confidently recount the situation in which she intervened with Tim, and the thought processes that accompanied this intervention. This teacher is not speculating about what she may have done; she is recalling what she perceives to have actually happened. She is describing the way in which she reacted to Tim's unsatisfactory first draft, by helping him to engage in a process of mental rehearsal before he attempts to draft his work. The confidence with which the teacher is able to make this claim, it is suggested, is a product of the manner in which she retrieves the information. The interviewer gives the informant freedom to explore the target situation in her own way. This is encouraged by the use of active listening techniques, avoidance of interrupting the informant and the use of paraphrase and 'mirroring' (i.e. repeating the informant's words back to him or her). All these techniques convey to informants the central significance that is attached to their definition of the situation as opposed to the researcher's definition. The information that the researcher seeks only comes forth when the interviewee is able to locate a route to the sought after information that leads from the landmark features of the target situation, which are (for whatever reason) already prominent in the interviewee's recollections of the situation.

*Authenticity*
The process of gradual build up and elaboration of informants' recollections, exemplified above, not only acts as an effective mnemonic for the informant; it also helps the researcher to have confidence in the authenticity of the interview data that are collected in this way. The researcher's gentle probing of informants does not suggest possible answers, it suggests possible starting points for recollection. This, coupled with the already stated measures for helping informants to feel valued and respected, along with the interviewer's avoidance of interruption and the use of active listening strategies, contributes to a situation in which the substantive content of the interview is directed by the interviewee. The interviewer's contribution is to provide an 'agenda' (Powney and Watts 1987) that directs the attention of interviewees to broad areas of experience; the detailed structure, however, is supplied by the interviewee. As the interviewees proceed through increasingly elaborate recollections, we are able to detect interrelationships within and between the elements recalled, which are complex and consistent and therefore unlikely to be contrived.

An example of this is provided by Zoe, whose account of a lesson is a model of logical consistency. She recalls the 'surface features' of the lesson as follows: 'Erm, well, you were learning about verbs, but you had a story board. You had to make up a story . . . in our groups. And everyone had to put verbs and things in it, and make it quite specific, and write a paragraph about it.' The stimulus material for the task is a photograph:

'I think it was quite a hard one to do, as well. Cos it was just two people walking up some stairs.' The surface features of the lesson, then, are the writing task, the stimulus material and the perceived difficulty of the task. Zoe's detailed account of the learning that she engaged in during the lesson consists, in essence, of an elaboration of how she completed the task and overcame the perceived difficulties. She describes her initial approach to the task:

> Er, well, I looked at it [the picture]; thought what they were doing, and what it looked like, in the stairs in the darkness. Erm, then I had to go and find the thesaurus. And because it was a dark picture I thought: 'dark'. So I looked up 'dark'. I chose a word from there, and used that instead. I did it like that.

The researcher then probes a little further into the cognitive processes that accompanied these events:

*I:*   Now, when you were doing this, what was going on in your head? What were you actually thinking about, when you were actually writing this?

*Zoe:*  Erm. I was just thinking what it would feel like to be actually going up the stairs; how it would feel. How warm it was; cold. What the stairs – the noise they made. Erm . . .

*I:*   So, were you imagining you were actually in the picture yourself? What it would really be like to be those people?

*Zoe:*  Yes.

*I:*   And then, how did you turn it into words?

*Zoe:*  Well, I just said it in one sentence: 'it was dark – old stairs – two people.' Then I sort of changed the words around, and split it into sentences . . .

*I:*   Did you actually say the words?

*Zoe:*  I wrote them down. Then I swapped them round for better words: more descriptive words.

*I:*   How did you decide on 'better'?

*Zoe:*  Well, I looked up 'dark' in the thesaurus, and it had other words meaning the same thing, and I chose one from there. And then I made it like into one sentence, and then I split it up into smaller sentences. Made it easier to say.

*I:*   Now when you made it descriptive, did you feel that it was important or better to make it descriptive, than the way you'd written it in the first place?

*Zoe:*  I think it was better because it made you feel as though you were in the picture. Cos if you just say: 'two people walking up a dark stairs', it's not very descriptive or anything.

*I:*   So is it more enjoyable to read then?

*Zoe:* I think that you actually feel that you are there. I like reading like that.

*I:* Ah, so you were thinking something about your own reading?

*Zoe:* Yes. I like reading things like that. I know that some of my friends do as well.

*I:* So you were trying to write something that you would like to read?

*Zoe:* Yes.

*I:* Was there anything that happened – you said about the thesaurus – that helped you? And you've said how your thinking – the way you visualized it. Did you visualize it? Did you actually see in your mind what was happening?

*Zoe:* Sort of . . . I suppose so . . .

*I:* But not quite?

*Zoe:* . . . At the beginning I didn't, but then sort of like when I was thinking which word to use – cos some of them have got different meanings – I sort of pictured then.

Zoe shows quite clearly how her written work on this occasion develops through a number of key strategic stages. (a) She begins with a description of the picture, which she writes in an unstructured form. (b) She consults the thesaurus for a more effective ('descriptive') vocabulary. (c) She assesses the words suggested in the thesaurus against the criteria of their effectiveness in portraying the scene as she visualizes it. (d) She constructs sentences, using the selected words. (e) She refines her sentence structure according to a criterion of readability ('made it easier to say') and on the basis of a calculation of audience response ('I like reading like that. I know that some of my friends do as well').

It is difficult to devise hard criteria for judging the authenticity of these data. We cannot know whether or not the cognitive processes reported by Zoe are an accurate account of her actual interactive thought processes. However, the detail, precision and logical consistency of her account are impressive and strongly suggest authenticity. The care with which she corrects the interviewer's assumption that she used a strategy of visualization throughout the exercise suggests that she is striving for accuracy of recall rather than a simply plausible explanation. Similarly, her description of the way in which her use of the thesaurus precedes her visualization of the scene, rather than being a tool for representing an existing visualization, is an unexpected response, which is unlikely to be selected for its plausibility alone, simply because it is not an obvious explanation. The tendency, already noted, of staff and pupils to assert their constructions of events and processes over those of the researcher is also suggestive of an intention to recall authentic events with accuracy.

While we are striving, in our research approach, for recall of authentic cognitive events, we have to recognize that such recall, while always being theoretically possible, will not always be achieved, particularly in the confines of a time-limited interview. Some, if not most, of what our interviewees tell us will take the form of *post hoc* rationalization, and this is not necessarily an altogether bad thing. What is important is that where such rationalizations are given, they are authentic in the sense of being grounded in actual classroom events, and that they develop from the interviewee's perceptions of how, as a rule, they actually think and behave when they are teaching or learning.

In the examples quoted above, it is perhaps possible to distinguish tentatively between recalled cognitions and grounded rationalizations. While the recall is marked by clarity and decisiveness in the informants' accounts, rationalization is marked by tentativeness and lack of detail. In other words, it is the informants themselves who signal to us the status of their accounts. It is suggested that the researcher's effort to encourage authentic recall, through both direct requests and cognitive methods, sometimes has the secondary effect of motivating the informant to produce authentic as opposed to groundless or idealized rationalizations. Moreover, because the examples cited above contain convincing accounts of cognitive processes, we are led to believe that they are striving for authenticity.

In judging the authenticity of informants' responses we must not forget that they take place within a social context. We have already dealt with ways in which the interview setting and procedure can be controlled to minimize the imposition of researcher perceptions over those of informants. There is also, however, the all important social context of the classroom. We must acknowledge the validity of Nisbett and Wilson's (1977) assertion that individuals' perceptions of their own cognitions can be culturally determined. We must acknowledge, for example, that when pupils claimed that the lesson they had just had was concerned with learning about groupwork, they had been told by the teacher on a prior occasion that this lesson was going to be, among other things, concerned with fostering their groupwork skills. The teacher's planning notes state the following aims:

> [Reads] To finally tackle the problem of groupwork; to work together as a class; take responsibility for their decisions; to utilise the powers of groupwork to put together a group presentation. And then to write a booklet in appropriate formal style; to write imaginatively and accurately; to use all the stages in the writing process, as a group, and to produce individual link pieces for different audiences.
>
> (Ms Pitt)

In an interview the same teacher states:

> I showed them [a year 7 class] an OHP [visual aid], with some things on that I'd actually taken out of the National Curriculum, about

erm . . . various things about audience, speaking and listening and things. And we talked about how they'd got to set up their talk.

The teacher here is communicating to pupils the purpose and content of the lessons in an overt manner. It is not surprising, therefore, that pupils describe the lesson content in the same terms used by the teacher; after all, she has already told them what the lessons are about. So when pupils are making these claims, are they reporting their own cognitions or simply parroting the teacher's?

A possible answer to this question is that pupils are doing both things. It could be argued that the dominant culture of this classroom and this school (perhaps most schools) gives the teacher's definition of the situation particular prominence. Because the teacher has defined this lesson as being concerned with groupwork (among other things), the pupils may *believe* that what they did in the lesson must have had something to do with groupwork, and so recall cognitions that can be construed as relating to groupwork skills. This suggests interesting possibilities about the relationship between the social and cognitive aspects of schooling, by highlighting the way in which the pupils' knowledge about their own social and cognitive functioning is socially constructed. At the same time, in this situation, it might also be suggested that the pupils are having a certain view of the culture of the school reinforced, namely that teachers' definitions are paramount. In relation to the central concerns of this research, methodological issues about the authenticity and validity of pupils' accounts become intertwined with questions of the effectiveness and value of teacher action aimed at helping pupils by giving them a meta view of the teaching and learning process (see Wang and Walberg 1983; Biggs 1987).

Obviously, the culture of the school is interpreted in different ways, at different times, by different pupils. The convergence of teacher and pupil perceptions identified here may be transformed into a divergence, when pupils are disaffected from the formal goals of the school. This offers an interesting insight into the relationship between the cultural and psychological aspects of schooling, and indicates the closely intertwined nature of these two strands.

## The departmental context

The subject department is a very important unit in the organization of secondary schooling in the UK. This is reflected in the structure of the teaching profession, as it is in the design of the National Curriculum. Part of a teacher's professional identity is related to his or her departmental affiliation. While it would be presumptuous to make claims about the effects of departmental membership on the individual teacher's thinking, it is important to recognize that the departmental dimension *may* be significant in this respect. This is particularly important when we consider that a major aim of the National Curriculum is to produce a degree of standardization in respect of curriculum content. For this reason we sought to develop an understanding of the departmental context in which each of the teachers in our study operated.

Data on the departmental context were gathered from a variety of sources. First, interviews with heads of department were carried out prior to the comencement of the observational fieldwork. The focus of these interviews was the head of department's perceptions of the department. Heads of department were asked to comment on departmental issues that were of particular concern to them in their daily work. Not surprisingly, at the time we carried out our study the heads of department were pre-occupied with the requirements of the National Curriculum. These were often talked about in relation to the particular historical and contemporaneous context of the department.

In addition to interview data gathered from heads of department, other departmental members were interviewed, including those who were not involved in the observational study. Furthermore, observational data were gathered by the researcher from attendance at formal scheduled meetings, as well as from participant observation with teachers in informal settings (e.g. during breaks, between lessons, before and after school). In these circumstances the researcher recorded information that appeared to be pertinent to the research questions, such as references to discussions about teaching effectiveness and the impact of the National Curriculum on the department.

Departmental data that were gathered from participant observation were validated in interviews with teachers.

*Data analysis*

Interview transcripts were analysed using a form of recursive comparative analysis developed by Brown and McIntyre (1993). This involved a process by which the unfolding descriptive theories that emerge from the data are constantly tested and refined to take account of all relevant data. The analysis took the following form:

- reading a random sample of transcripts;
- identifying points of similarity and difference among these transcripts in relation to our research questions;
- generating theories describing emergent answers to research questions;
- testing theories against a new set of transcripts;
- testing new theories against transcripts already dealt with;
- carrying all existing theories forward to new transcripts;

- repeating the above processes until all data have been examined and all theories tested against all data.

## Summary and conclusion

In this chapter we have described the methodology we adopted when seeking data on teachers' and pupils' perceptions of effective teaching and learning. A major concern has been to underline the importance of a reflective approach in research of this type, and the need to develop systematic approaches that are related in a systematic way to the claims and intentions of the research.

We have identified a number of key procedures that we believe to be necessary in the collection of authentic data on informants' perceptions. These procedures can be thought of as a series of four steps which could be followed by researchers pursuing similar studies. The steps can be defined as follows.

Step 1: define desired relationships. Define the type of researcher–participant relationship that is most appropriate to the research questions that are to be addressed. This also requires the researcher to identify the type of persona that he or she wishes to present to the participants.

Step 2: negotiate access. Where possible, negotiate access by approaching potential informants informally, before seeking formal permission from senior school management or other higher institutional authority. This helps to ensure voluntary participation. Where this is not possible (e.g. with pupils), attempt to establish rapport with informants before engaging in fieldwork with them. At all times the researchers should be open with respondents about the research agenda and be prepared to deal with possible concerns and fears that they might have.

Step 3: select techniques. Select research techniques that maximize the potential for authentic responses. This will involve making efforts to ensure that the techniques chosen: (a) reflect needs defined in research questions; (b) are open enough to allow informants to express their own concerns; (c) are so designed that they motivate informants to be honest and accurate in their responses. In the current study these needs were met by combining participant observation with a programme of interviews. Informant style group, pair and individual interviews were employed in order to facilitate recall, in both their structure and timing.

Step 4: enact appropriate relationship. When beginning fieldwork and throughout the fieldwork period the researcher must behave towards participants in ways that are consistent with the aspirations set out in step 1. Efforts must be continually made to present and maintain the appropropriate persona (see references to 'empathy', 'unconditional positive regard' and 'congruence').

# 3/ *The National Curriculum context*

In this chapter we begin to report and discuss some of the substantive findings of the research project. The specific focus of this chapter will be the impact of the National Curriculum (NC) on teachers' thinking and classroom practice. The NC is an important focus because it was newly introduced into secondary schools at the time of the research (1991–3). Key Stage 3 (KS3) English had been introduced in 1990, while KS3 history was introduced in 1991. This fact meant that practical concerns about the interpretation and implementation of the NC were prominent in the minds of teachers, thus providing us with a unique opportunity to explore the ways in which they responded to and dealt with this imposed innovation as it happened.

In this chapter we will describe the impact of the NC as it was perceived by the teachers in our study in the following terms:

- the ways in which teachers of history and English responded to and interpreted the NC;
- the ways in which teachers with different subject ideologies responded to and interpreted the NC;
- the ways in which teachers' thinking about individual differences among pupils interacted with their responses to the NC;
- teachers' perceptions of the effects of the NC on their classroom practice;
- the perceived impact of the NC on subject departments.

In Chapter 1 we outlined some of the background debates associated with the introduction of the NC in English and history. The positions which we outlined there were of course those adopted by people who were vocal in the NC debate in the professional and academic media. It would be a mistake to assume that practising teachers adhered in a consensual way to any of these positions. It was, however, against the background of these public debates that we were seeking access to teachers' authentic thinking about effective teaching in their own practice. As will be seen, the teachers of our study varied greatly in the degree to which they concerned themselves with these debates.

This chapter is devoted to the initial responses to the NC of teachers in the present study. It will be shown that there was a wide range of responses of individual teachers to the curriculum, and that differences in response can be related to individual differences among teachers in terms of the strength and nature of their views of their subject and their professional purpose. There were also interesting differences between English and history teachers' responses. English teachers who articulated a clear sense of their aims as English teachers seemed confident and enthusiastic in their response, showing a willingness and ability to *appropriate* the NC in terms of their existing values. English teachers with a less clearly articulated sense of purpose tended to express a sense of being threatened and overwhelmed by the NC. Members of the former group sometimes seemed to act as mediators between the curriculum and their less confident colleagues, thus creating a genuine departmental response to the NC. This pattern of departmental mediation, however, only took place within departments where heads or senior members of the department were both confident and enthusiastic in their response to the NC, and imposed a strong leadership style. There was a more fragmented response in departments without such leadership. By and large, however, there was a positive response to the NC English, because it was often perceived by teachers to be associated with progressive practice in their subject. By contrast, history teachers in the present study had a less positive view of the NC in their subject. Their major complaints centred on what they saw as the excessive weight of content that the NC required them to deliver to pupils. This concern led many of them to become preoccupied with the need to 'cover' the prescribed content at the expense of their preferred styles of teaching. For history teachers, then, the NC was often perceived to be at odds with their notions of effective teaching.

## The ways in which teachers responded to and interpreted the National Curriculum

### English

#### The English units

Two teachers from each of four English departments were involved in the first phase of our study. One pair of teachers was studied for a single six-hour unit of teaching each, with their respective year 7 classes (i.e. pupils aged 11–12 years), in the final term of the 1990–1 academic year. The remaining English teachers were each studied for a four-hour unit in each of the three terms of the 1991–2 academic year.

Units taught included the following topics.

- Short story form and structure (six units).
- Poetry: lyric poems.
- Poetry: the ballad (two units).
- Autobiography (two units).
- Knowledge about language (KAL): dialect and standard English.
- KAL: the origins of the English language.
- Listening skills.
- Preparing a public speech (two units).
- Pre twentieth-century literature: Shakespeare's *The Tempest.*
- The novel: *The Eighteenth Emergency.*
- The play form (two units).

In practice, teachers did not always stick exclusively to the intended unit. In addition to allowing the occasional digression, the beginnings of scheduled units were sometimes devoted to finishing off a previous unit's work, and the ends were sometimes given over to the beginning of a new unit if the scheduled unit was felt to be exhausted. By and large, however, the sheduled units took up most of the time that had been allocated for them.

*English teachers' responses to the National Curriculum*
Individually the English teachers in this study expressed a generally positive view of the NC in 1991. One head of department summed up feelings implied by others when he said with enthusiasm that the NC had helped to 'take the ad hoccery out of English teaching'. For this head of department the NC has helped with the

> spring cleaning of practice [that is] having a look at what we're doing and tightening up on organization and all. In that respect I see the National Curriculum as being very beneficial, because it's made us all think long and hard again about how we are structuring work.

This head of English, along with one other of the four studied, described the NC as a valuable management tool, giving weight to his personal commitment to certain aspects of English, and thus helping him to influence the practice of some of his more conservative or unadventurous colleagues. However, he does qualify his enthusiasm when he draws a distinction between the report of the English working party and the final curriculum document produced by the government:

> When I say the national curriculum, half the time we're talking about the Cox Report [the report of the English working party] . . . after it was published I did think in many ways it was quite a liberal document,

because it did talk about all those things which should be happening, and it did give a high place to media and it did give a high place to oral work.

For many of these teachers the NC provided a welcome map of their subject. There were three main patterns of response under this heading. The first is represented by the head of department referred to in the previous paragraph: for these teachers the NC confirmed their view of English as embracing a wide range of activities, including media studies and oracy. The NC map was seen as less of a benefit to their personal practice than as a valuable aid to influencing the thinking and practice of some of their colleagues. These teachers can be seen to have a clear sense of the nature and purpose of their subject as well as clear views about how it should be organized and delivered. A second pattern of response finds teachers welcoming a curriculum map which helps them to manage what they perceive to be a vast and complex subject, by identifying areas of study and teaching objectives. In this pattern the NC is essentially a planning aid: 'What I did this year – and what I shall probably do this summer – is: I've sort of sat down; took the areas (roughly); the different types of writing, types of reading et cetera [that] you're supposed to cover . . . Then I planned out each term, what I had to do.' As in the first pattern, the teacher has a clear sense of the complex nature of the subject, but has less of a clear idea about how to deliver it. The third pattern of response welcomes the curriculum map not only as an organizer but as a prompt and source of ideas that stretch the teacher's conception of the subject: 'I quite like it because it's a checklist for me, because I know I can slip into what's easy for me . . . And it makes me try – or has made me try – different things. And I think that's a good thing.' In this response pattern the teacher has less of a clear idea about the nature of the subject, and is inclined to be conservative and unconfident about attempting new challenges. In this pattern the teacher welcomes the NC as a liberating influence, a provider of guidance and opportunities for the development of new skills and a way out of a professional rut.

An important aspect linking the first and third response patterns is the role of the department. For heads of departments and members of departments who are keen to disseminate innovatory practice, the NC provides a focus for the departmental effort. In order to ensure that Key Stage appropriate attainment targets are met it is necessary for members of departments to consult with one another and collaborate in their planning. For the sake of continuity and coherence, teachers need to know what their colleagues have done and are doing. The innovatory heads of department are able to use this forum to promote their preferred approaches. This level of response is welcomed by teachers representing the other response patterns:

I think the national curriculum is very positive. Well, I've enjoyed doing it. Just the sharing of ideas, the booklets that have been produced. It's allowed you to use the ideas that are there with the groups that you have. And the fact that you are all producing a booklet, or the fact that we talk regularly about what we've done [that] has worked [has also been good] . . . you're not working on your own. And each half term we have a target.

In departments where there is less of a collaborative approach there tend to be inconsistencies and even conflicts in the manner in which the National Curriculum is interpreted. These conflicts are often rooted in differences in subject ideology and will be described in greater detail in the following section.

On the negative side almost all of the English teachers involved in this study expressed a variety of serious reservations about the assessment component of the National Curriculum. As one head of department put it:

I've got big problems with the assessment. I think the assessment is inadequate and I think it's illogical almost . . . I think it's impossible to show up language development in the crude way that it's being suggested [in the NC] . . . I don't think you can tick boxes with language development.

This teacher's concern reflects an actively critical stance toward the National Curriculum. The teacher's concern with the NC's structuring of the subject for pedagogical assessment implies a rejection of the 'teacher as pedagogue' model (see Chapter 1) that is implicit in the NC. For this teacher, assessment practices have to be informed by a thorough understanding of the nature of the subject knowledge and the way in which it is learned.

Another commonly expressed view was that the need to maintain an ongoing record of each pupil's progress in terms of the statements of attainment was cumbersome as well as being a waste of time. It was felt that the statements of attainment were often imprecise, or simply meaningless. For example, several teachers remarked on the phrase 'read a range of fiction', which appears as a statement of attainment at levels 6, 7, 8, 9 and 10. The complaint here relates to the imprecision of the statement in its failure to specify the expected difference between the same attainment at the different levels. As one teacher states, somewhat stridently:

We're not afraid of the NC in this school, simply because we're already doing it. And all we have to do was then find the right box to tick. That's what I object to. And very strongly! And the strand and the levels . . . To me they're not progressive. Sometimes you think: 'What are you asking here? What do you want me to do?' And certainly a lot of the stuff we've actually presented to the children, they've done it, but whether or not they are capable of repeating it, that's in the lap of the gods. Who knows? And I haven't got time to go over it again just to make sure I can put a cross instead of half a line in that box. So I hate, loathe and detest that part of it!

Furthermore, it was felt that the assignment of rigid 'levels' to children's performance would have a negative effect on the self-esteem of pupils who were assigned relatively lower levels. It was felt that this process would undermine some of the advantages of mixed ability grouping, which enables teachers to emphasize the importance of individual progress over competition with peers.

The greatest concern, in relation to assessment, was voiced about the proposed end of Key Stage Standard Assessment Tasks (SATs). Although proposals as to the precise nature of these tests were not at this time available, certain characteristics of the tests were known, and were a source of disquiet to English teachers. A major concern expressed by all the English teachers was that the tests would take the form of formal paper and pencil examinations. There were two difficulties associated with this.

First, the style of testing would be in conflict with preferred and established methods of testing. Since the introduction of the GCSE, in the late 1980s, English departments had eschewed final written examinations in favour of continual assessment. All the English departments in this study had abandoned end of year examinations. This meant that both teachers and pupils would have to make fairly speedy readjustments, which would include addressing issues of examination technique. More importantly, certain key aspects of the post-GCSE English curriculum were felt to be incompatible with terminal examination testing. The most often quoted example here is that of the drafting process. For all the English teachers involved in the research, the drafting process was seen as essential to the production of a finished piece of writing. They all devoted a considerable amount of time and effort to convincing pupils of the benefits of drafting.

Second, those aspects of English which were least amenable to terminal testing would be neglected. Thus, in spite of the fact that drafting was referred to in the NC statements of attainment, it was felt that the failure of the SATs to test this aspect of writing would relegate it to a level of relative unimportance. Teachers would inevitably be influenced to 'teach to the tests', since pupil attainment in their subject was going to be publicly judged in terms of test results. This, it was feared, might lead to a regressive and narrowly focused view of the subject, which would undo many of the positive effects of the NC:

> what I worry about [is that] if we prepare the children for very crude pencil and paper tests . . . English teachers might go back to *The Art of English*. You know, people might think, in desperation, 'well, the

best thing I can do is just get *The Art of English* book out of the cupboard and just plod through it.'

Here the concern is with a possible return to a style of English teaching that is associated in the minds of these teachers with the period prior to the advent of GCSE. The emphasis of such teaching is on comprehension tests and mechanical grammar exercises. The majority of these teachers saw such a mechanistic approach to English as highly reductive, ignoring what they see as key aspects of English. These key aspects emphasize the value of pupils' self-exploration and self-expression. As one teacher illustrates,

> Under this little top sheet there's a rough draft of some notes, and there's a neat draft. And you can talk about the language development that's taken place in the production of that unit of work . . . That is very interesting – very stimulating for the kids to do. They love to do it. It's breeding – I think here – a generation of writers who are vigorous and honest and interesting . . . But if we're going to do a series of pen and paper tests, then there might be pressure put upon us to abandon all that practice and say, 'well, what we've actually got to do is get these kids prepared for these tests. These secretarial skill tests.'

This is not to say that the teachers wish to avoid the teaching of grammar and the technical aspects of writing. While they vary in the degree to which they choose to approach these as discrete topics, they all agree that these are aspects of English that should be addressed by English teachers.

Some teachers welcome the emphasis on formal basic writing skills, such as the use of punctuation and grammar, and intend to address these in specific 'language' lessons. Others prefer to integrate this work within the context of pupils' broader development as writers:

> The way we use drafting in the department is to develop children's language skills, because it forces a teacher to sit down with an individual at some point in the lesson, even if it is only for a minute . . . and say: 'Now look, I've had a look at your rough draft and can we talk about these possible changes?' Or to show them in the context of their own writing, which is always the key for me . . . You can always show them where they've made a grammatical error. So if they're not using the apostrophe – you know, rather than give them a test out of a book – you know, a complete abstraction of their own experience – you can say: 'Look . . . you've written this story in which there's dialogue between . . . a joy rider and a policeman . . . and you've kind of adopted a particular style of writing for this joy rider, and you're . . . dropping aitches – which is fine . . . but there's a convention to go

with that, and it's this. And here's how it can operate in your writing.'
So you're addressing those secretarial skills of sentencing and gram-
matical aspects of the writing, while you're talking about improving a
piece and while he's talking about redrafting.

The consensus among these teachers, then, was that certain aspects of
the assessment and testing procedures were likely to undermine positive
aspects of the NC attainment targets. This was seen as being because (a)
important aspects of the NC could not be effectively tested by the proposed
methods, and (b) the teaching required to prepare children for the tests
was likely to be restricted in content, as a direct result of the testing
format. Both the positive and the negative criticisms of the NC were framed
in terms of teachers' theories of assessment and their knowledge of their
subject.

*Subject ideology and responses to the National Curriculum*
Although the teachers who were the main focus of the study were in broad
agreement as to the merits and demerits of the NC, there were variations
in their responses which seemed to be linked with issues relating to
dfferences in subject ideology.

When one is considering differences in teachers' subject ideologies,
there are two important dimensions of which to take account. First is the
degree to which the individual is conscious of having a distinctive ideology, and the degree to which this consciously influences his or her approach
to the NC, and second is the ideology itself. Of the eight English teachers
involved in this study, two could be said to be firmly committed to a consciously articulated and strong ideology of their subject, which they were
aware of influencing their response to the NC and their teaching. The
majority of the teachers (five) held less consciously articulated ideologies,
that could be inferred from their talk about their teaching and the
NC. The eighth teacher presented a much weaker sense of ideological
commitment.

The two teachers who communicated the strongest sense of a subject
ideology were also those who were the most critical of the NC. Both
shared the view that the study of English can be a source of empowerment
for pupils. One of the major benefits of such study can be to foster in
pupils a set of skills that enables them to understand the ways in which
media (including literature) can contrive to manipulate the thoughts and
feelings of an audience:

Teaching them how to read ... is very central to English teaching,
because it spins off into all sorts of other things. I mean ... well it's
not just a spin off – it illuminates and is reinforced by lots of other
reading skills, like reading advertisements, well, reading the media

generally. But I don't differentiate between reading books and reading the media, which seems to be one of the things that the NC does do. I would exert or apply the same kind of suspicion to literature as the NC suggests we should apply to the media.

With regard to writing: 'the other side of reading is, you know, if you're being manipulated by the text, then how can you create a text which manipulates others?' While sharing similar views of the empowering potential of English study, the second teacher placed greater emphasis on the personal growth aspect of the subject, seeing the study of literature, composition and drama as a vehicle enabling pupils to explore and articulate their emotional responses. In both cases, however, these teachers were positive in their responses to the NC, in relation to those aspects of it which endorsed their ideologies. They were also critical of the extent to which they felt the NC to imply a reductive or 'secretarial' view of English. This they felt to be potentially threatening to their desire to foster critical approaches in their students. These views were often associated with reservations about NC assessment arrangements (see above), and the fear that differently motivated colleagues might opt to 'teach to the tests' only.

The majority of the teachers (five) fell into the category of implicit ideology. Unlike the two teachers with explicit ideologies, these teachers tended not to make claims about the long-term effects on pupils of the study of English. They tended to focus almost solely on the immediate subject skills that were being addressed in their lessons. Thus when, for example, one of these teachers referred to the importance of 'critical thinking' as a skill, she did this within the context of the unit of work that was being studied, and did not relate this to the wider social purpose of the subject. These teachers tended to come across as ideologically neutral in their responses to the NC. Although they identified practical difficulties in interpreting the NC statements of attainment, they tended to be less questioning of the validity of the NC than the more ideologically conscious teachers. An exception to this was one of the teachers from the pilot phase of the project (interviewed in the summer term of 1991). He was critical of the NC on the grounds that it might interfere with the social relationships which exist between teachers and students of English, and which he felt to be unique to English in schools. He saw English as a major vehicle for personal and social education, and felt that the NC might be too content heavy to allow this to continue.

The eighth teacher appeared to be more concerned with the mechanics of implementing the NC in English than the others. This teacher expressed unreserved enthusiasm for the NC, because she saw it as broadening the scope of her teaching. She also welcomed the opportunities she perceived to be created by the NC for learning from her colleagues their ways of teaching to the requirements of the NC.

*Individual differences among pupils and teachers' responses to the*
*National Curriculum*
There was a strong commitment shared by the majority of the English
teachers to mixed ability teaching, particularly in KS3. A variety of reasons
were given for this. Some teachers felt that children's abilities were too
often judged on the basis of their literacy skills, and that performance and
progress in English did not have to depend on these skills. Teachers were
often able to cite examples of pupils who were technically slow learners,
with low reading ages and poor writing skills, who could out-perform their
peers conceptually, and who were, as a consequence, a valuable presence
in the mixed ability setting. The fear was expressed, however, that the
perceived emphasis on the technical skills of reading and writing, and the
demands of end of Key Stage pencil and paper tests, would have the effect
of over-emphasizing the importance of literacy skills at the expense of
orality. This, it was feared, would undermine the so-called 'weaker' pupils
and demotivate them, especially when this was accompanied by the assignment of levels.

There was another prominent view expressed, which related to the
importance of 'enjoyment' in English study. An important aim of the year
7 English course according to these teachers was to stimulate enthusiasm
for the study of English: 'I want to teach them that English is interesting
and dynamic; that it's got so many off-shoots; so many facets you can
explore.' This involved, for all the teachers at different times, giving pupils
tasks that were principally for their enjoyment, such as the reading of a
particular text, or the discussion of an item of interest. In these circumstances, evidence of pupil participation and enjoyment were sufficient
criteria of effectiveness for teachers. Similarly, this was related to allowing
pupils to develop their own lines of interest. Teachers felt that where
pupils requested the opportunity to develop their own piece of work (e.g.
to write a story in response to a poem that had been read), this should be
encouraged, since it showed enthusiasm for the subject and initiative that
would hasten their development of certain skills by capitalizing on their
motivations. It was feared, however, that the mechanistic impulses of the
NC would constrain teachers to adhere to rigid plans which would pre-
clude opportunities for pupil initiative of this type. It was also felt that the
demand to cover a prescribed range of content would add to this effect.
This forcing of the pace would inevitably operate against the interests of
pupils who were considered to be 'weaker', who might be demotivated by
intense pressure.

This is not to say that teachers were blithely 'giving in' to these perceived
pressures. Rather they witnessed a tension between the impulses of the
NC, as they perceived them, and their own views of best practice. Central
here was the issue of pupil self-esteem, and the need to have space in
order to cater for individual differences between pupils.

*f the National Curriculum on teachers' classroom practice*

vould appear to be something of a dissonance between teachers'
ions of the effects of the NC on their classroom practice and their
experience of those effects. When asked directly to describe the effects of
the NC on their classroom teaching they most often claimed that their
teaching had not been affected by the NC. They most often claimed that
the NC was an endorsement for the kind of teaching that they had already
been doing prior to its advent. The exception to this was the teacher
referred to above who appeared to be without an obvious ideological
commitment. She attributes to the NC an improved sense of continuity in
her teaching:

*Q:* So have you tackled this unit in a way that's different to the way that
you might have tackled it before the NC came along?
*A:* Yeah. Maybe I was sustaining it; taking it further, and building up ideas
rather than just reading the odd play and writing about it. [The NC]
makes us focus on extending ideas that are already there . . . it does make
you, I suppose, more thorough in a way. [And] it does make you do
more long term planning . . . In the past I might have thought, 'Gosh!
We haven't done any play reading.' I might have dipped in . . . Just the
fact of reading aloud as an introduction . . . and then perhaps gone on
to some play writing without so much preparation, I think.

The themes raised here of greater continuity between the component
parts of a unit, more detailed and thorough planning and more thorough
preparation of pupils are echoed in the classroom practice of other teachers too. There was a commonly asserted view that every task set had to be
justified in terms of learning objectives and NC attainment targets, whereas
prior to the NC there was a greater tendency to offer year 7 pupils tasks
for the sake of the experience of doing the task. Similarly, prior to the NC,
teachers felt less constraint in terms of time, and would be less inclined
to force the pace of task completion. There was also more opportunity in
the pre-NC period to 'go off on tangents', in terms of classroom learning
activities, that were dictated by pupil interests or other emergent factors.

Once again, however, there were variations among the teachers in relation to the degree to which the NC appeared to have affected their
practice, with the more ideologically explicit teachers tending to show the
least signs of change. This can be attributed to the fact that they appeared
to have approached their teaching with a clearer sense of the outcomes
they were aiming for, and in a more structured manner than the others
prior to the NC.

A major effect on all the teachers was the increased detail of their
proactive planning. In some cases this was facilitated by the practice of
departmental planning. This involved teachers producing 'modules' or
'units' of work that were designed to meet the requirements of specific

NC Attainment Targets (ATs). The degree to which these units were prescriptive varied both between units within departments and between departments as a whole. At their most prescriptive, units were broken down lesson by lesson; at their least prescriptive, they provided a series of possible activities that were directly related to ATs. On the whole the teachers were uncomfortable with the extremely prescriptive units; and whether or not they stuck to the letter of the preordained unit, all the English teachers were constrained to teach each particular topic within a specified period. Their ways of meeting this demand involved, for all of them, planning more rigorously than they had been used to doing prior to the NC. The explanation for this was that they had to be sure of covering the specified topic within a given period, often owing to the limited availability of resources. Prior to the advent of the NC teachers felt that they had more latitude in terms of whether or not they covered a particular topic in year 7 or whether they left it to a later stage. The emphasis on tight planning was believed to have led to a reduction in opportunities for spontaneous diversions stimulated by pupil interests (see above). This was a source of regret to many teachers.

Associated with the detailed individual and departmental planning were the broadening of some teachers' teaching repertoires and, in some cases, shifts in emphasis with regard to the relative stress placed on different aspects of the English curriculum. For some teachers this meant a vast reduction in the amount of time given to the study of literary texts. Teachers who had formerly based virtually all of their teaching on a series of class readers (usually novels) found that they were only able to teach a single novel throughout the year, and were now required to employ a variety of starting points, such as the use of drama texts, non-literary media and poetry. Similarly, the impetus of the NC 'strands' required a balance to be struck between the use of writing, reading, speaking and listening. For some teachers, this meant a shift in emphasis to create a balance. For some teachers this created a sense of discomfort. An extreme example of this is provided by a teacher who was not one of the main participants in the study, but who was a member of one of the departments:

> Personally, I find the NC irritating and inhibiting. I've been teaching for 24 years, I think now. And so everyone develops a teaching style of one's own, and I am personally not happy about them looking over my shoulder to see what I should be doing, according to the dictum, or body rather, which has decided what ought to be taught. For me personal teaching style is very important . . .
>
>     I mean, for instance, over the question of oral work: setting it is very difficult. And it's not something that I'm particularly happy about. I've never been happy with it. I enjoy oral work, but it's something I prefer to do spontaneously. And I do all the things one's expected to

do, like pair work and group work, and I've always been doing that. But the idea one has to set it up in a particular way, in order to assess it, rather irks me. [But] I have constantly, I think, to make sure that I cover that, because it's laid down in the NC.

This teacher regrets that he has less opportunity than he had prior to the NC to devote to his own enthusiasms within English:

Perhaps it's a failing of mine – that I'm too narrow in what I expect to be doing as a teacher. Nevertheless, I do strongly feel that a personal commitment, a personal teaching style, a personal enthusiasm is acutely vital . . . I just feel that certain demands of the NC cut right across that.

This teacher cites his own enthusiasms as being for literature and creative writing. He mourns what he sees as the diminished opportunities for pupil story writing, and the lack of room to respond to pupils' immediate concerns and interests. He attributes these losses to the over-prescriptiveness of the NC. He describes the personal effects of this somewhat dramatically: 'What has died in me is often what I am enthusiastic about.'

A positive effect of the NC on classroom practice was that it encouraged teachers to share with pupils the aims of lessons and units. Whereas, prior to the NC, teachers would have stressed mechanical and practical requirements when introducing a task, after the introduction of the NC teachers were more inclined to add references to the planned learning outcomes, sometimes with direct reference to NC statements of attainment.

*The perceived impact of the National Curriculum on subject departments*
As has already been pointed out, the advent of the NC seems, initially at least, to have given the departments a sense of shared purpose. The requirement of the NC that a standardized curriculum be taught at KS3 led to the wholesale production of detailed plans for delivering the curriculum. In order for the appropriate attainment targets and statements of attainment to be addressed, and for a balance to be created in the delivery of the 'strands' of the NC, detailed planning was made necessary at the departmental level. This was orchestrated by heads of department in conjunction with newly appointed KS3 coordinators, whose role it was to monitor and facilitate the development of modules that were designed in accordance with NC requirements. This was in part a response to the need to share limited resources between classes, so that, for example, all groups could get the opportunity to study a particular text. It was also a means of ensuring that all teachers covered the prescribed ground. Prior to the NC there had been in all of the departments studied considerable lattitude and individualism in terms of the curriculum delivered in year 7. It would seem that this had continued to be the case further up the schools. As a

result, teachers had tended to concentrate on their specialist interests and, in some cases, to neglect least favoured areas of the English curriculum. The NC, therefore, was a force making some teachers address neglected areas of the curriculum. The effects of neglect included a lack of confidence in addressing certain topics, which was dealt with in some departments by the sharing of teaching approaches and the pooling of resources. Most teachers welcomed this, as providing opportunities to develop their own skills, and, in some cases, as providing a platform from which to educate their colleagues.

*History*

Five history teachers were studied. One was studied for a single unit during the pilot phase of the project (in the third term of 1990–1). Two history teachers from one department were studied for three units each throughout the academic year 1991–2. Two further history teachers from a third history department were studied for a single unit in the first term of the academic year 1992–3. It is important to note that we experienced significant difficulties in recruiting history teachers for the study. Refusal to participate was often justified in relation to the difficulties that teachers were experiencing in implementing the NC, which entered KS3 for the first time in 1991–2, the year of our main study. These problems, compared with the relative ease we experienced in recruiting English teachers, might be attributed to two main factors.

First, history departments are invariably smaller than English departments. This means that the administrative burdens tend to be heavier for individual teachers. It also meant that with a given department there were fewer people to choose from when trying to recruit research participants. If a single member of a history department did not seem to be keen to be involved in the research, this often made proceeding with that department unviable, because of an insufficient number of available teachers.

Second, the timing of our approaches to the departments was bad. In addition to the workload implications of the newly introduced NC, there is a confidence issue. Our experience with the English teachers indicated that their confidence in their ability to cope with the NC grew with their experience of handling it. They often claimed that initially they had held many fears about the nature of the curriculum which were allayed during their first year of working through it. At the time of our initial approaches the history teachers were a year behind their English counterparts. Although the small-scale nature of our study makes generalizations impossible, it is true to say that we detected a gradual growth in confidence of the history teachers we studied in the first year of implementation, and that the teachers we studied in the second year shared something of the English teachers' sense of having 'domesticated' the National Curriculum, and of feeling unthreatened by it.

*The history units*
The following history units were taught:

- The nature of historical evidence.
- The rise of the Roman Empire.
- The legacy of the Roman Empire.
- The extent of the Roman Empire.
- The nature and use of primary and secondary sources in history.
- The Peasants' Revolt.
- Background to the Norman Conquest.
- The Black Death.

It should be pointed out that the history teachers, like the English teachers, tended to plan their work in termly and half-termly blocks. These unit titles were provided in interviews with the teachers, and are intended to refer to the four- to six-hour research units that we were there to study. It is interesting to note, therefore, that six of the eight units are titled with reference to the historical content, while two of the titles refer to specific historical skills. The three departments studied planned their termly and half-termly programme around the NC programmes of study, and took their titles from the historical periods referred to there. The teacher who titled his unit 'the nature of historical evidence' was studied in the term before KS3 history officially started (i.e. the third term of 1990–1). He was one of two teachers who made no reference to NC programmes of study in his teaching. Rather, he based the topic on (a) a set of published materials which dealt with issues of 'evidence' in the context of a fictionalized mystery story, concerning the victim of a fatal road accident, and (b) a pamphlet dealing with the Tollund Man story. The second teacher, whose unit is titled 'the nature and use of primary and secondary sources in history', was studied in the first term of 1992–3. This deviation from the NC was part of an introductory course which the department delivered to its new year 7 classes in an attempt to overcome the difficulties that might arise from what the head of department saw as the somewhat patchy preparation that pupils received for KS3 history in the primary school.

*History teachers' responses to the National Curriculum*
None of the history teachers were hostile to the NC in their subject. However, while some English teachers positively welcomed the content of the NC, for the ways in which it was perceived to endorse a broad and diverse view of their subject, the most positive responses from the history teachers in the present study were somewhat more reserved. As with English,

some teachers welcomed the structure and direction that the NC provides for their teaching:

> I think the NC has actually made me . . . look [at] what I am actually doing: what am I actually trying to teach here? . . . Whereas I would perhaps in the past have seen a piece of work in a book; a set of questions in a book, and thought, 'well, that's quite useful', and just set it to go away and do it, without actually thinking, 'well have they actually got the skills to do these questions?'
>
> . . . I suppose that you always . . . taught certain topics in certain ways, and it's just habit . . . The NC has made me think a lot more about what I'm doing and why . . . I think when you've been teaching a number of years, a jolt like this is very good. I'm very happy with it. I'm very pleased with the way it's all going really. And I feel I can see progress.
>
> (Head of department (HoD) 2, 10 April 1992)

In contrast to this head of department, a second head of department describes in retrospect his initial fears that the NC would undermine the scope for individuality among history teachers, and thereby threaten the quality of teaching in some cases:

> I think different schools approach historical topics in different ways, and often using the particular skills and ideas that an individual group of teachers have. And to take that away, I think, is a great shame. In fact, I might say that I think most teachers are very worried that the NC would do that across the board. It would be something that would remove the individual teacher's particular preferences or attributes. And I think the way it's been designed has safeguarded that as best as possible, in a quite positive way. The amount of prescribed things that we need to do are not onerous as such. What is onerous is the amount of content that we're expected to cover in the core topics, and the guidance that we've had on that has also been rather vague I think.
>
> (HoD 3, 8 October 1992)

It is important to note that this teacher's positive remarks about the NC are tempered by complaints about the weight of content that the NC requires history teachers to cover. This complaint is echoed by all the history teachers in the study:

> If you think about the time frame we've got to do this in: we've got to do three history study units in a year; we've got five periods a week for half a year. So it's basically six weeks per study unit. That's 30 single periods. Most of them are taught by double periods. So it's going to be: boom, boom, boom, boom! Straight, y'know.
>
> (HoD 1, June 1991)

I'm feeling under pressure about getting through it all ... I know that I can't afford to give more than this week to Thomas Becket, and in many ways that's too much, because we've only got two weeks, so I'm going to have to devise ways of dealing with Magna Carta and the Peasants' Revolt fairly speedily ... we're supposed to be doing the origins of parliament, and Scotland and Wales, and the legacy of the Middle Ages. I just, you know – how do I get all that done in such a short time?

(HoD 2, 8 April 1992)

The NC is going to force us into a situation where we have to cut corners in terms of time, by cutting corners in terms of the quality of work we want them to produce ... What's going to be sacrificed? Can we make a big enough stand? Can we make a persuasive enough argument to say, when push comes to shove, we have to go for quality of work rather than coverage of the NC?

(Teacher 2, dept 3, 5 November 1992)

The last quotation refers to a problem recognized by four of the five teachers in the present study, namely that the pressure of time, imposed by the heavy content of the NC, will discourage teachers from employing adventurous and engaging teaching styles and encourage instead transmission styles of teaching. As another head of department put it: 'If it's going to be a question of teachers thinking, "well, we've run out of time now; we only have another two lessons, and we haven't covered this, this, this, and this," there's going to be a temptation for teachers to just lecture' (HoD 3, 8 October 1992). This in turn, it is feared, will lead to pupils producing superficial work of an inferior quality to that which can be produced when more time is granted for individual reflection and exploration.

Another concern expressed by teachers in department 3 (i.e. those studied in the second year of KS3 history), is the lack of logical progression in the assessment levels:

At borough meetings [i.e. meetings with other heads of history departments from within the same 'borough'] we've been through all the attainment targets and said how little they really do reflect progression. You know, there's ten levels on each of the attainment targets, and theoretically each level is a stage ahead of the one before, and it's very difficult to acknowledge that that's been well thought out. There's often a down turn progression, and in terms of the second attainment target, the difficulty seems to be grouped from about level three upwards to ten ... From level three the gap – the gulf – in terms of a mental and intellectual jump is absolutely phenomenal.

(HoD 3, 8 October 1992)

A related complaint, which echoes problems perceived by English teachers, concerns the uncertainties surrounding the assessment procedures. As the head of department 1 put it, somewhat facetiously, 'You'll find the SATs are totally different to the sorts of exercises you've been setting all the way through!' (Laughs.) Over a year later, the head of department 3 expressed a similar sense of uncertainty, and indicated how this causes planning difficulties:

It's been very difficult to plan a coordinated course, without being entirely sure how the assessment picture is going to be at the end of it. So we've had to work a little bit with rumours . . . And that has been a very considerable problem in fact. Because obviously it started last September. Not only did we want to plan for what we were going to be doing last year . . . but we also had an overall picture of the different NC topics that we'd do over KS3. And we came to a fairly satisfactory solution, in terms of what we wanted to do, which we thought created quite a broad and balanced course. Only to find that the marking/assessment strategy is going to make that very difficult to actually – and we also need to do a number of optional units. And the assessment strategy that I understand is going to take place is that there will be SATs . . . aimed at the spring term of year 9. And they will be on the core units, which means that logically, the last term of year 9 we'll have to be working on an option unit, and the chronological sequencing of the topics that we'd planned to do has been totally put out of order by that problem. Because our plans were to finish with core units which seemed to chronologically – logically – end at that point. And we've got problems there. We're going to have to decide to do something out of chronological sequence . . . But you see, even now, we're only going on something that's little better than hearsay.

(HoD 3, 8 October 1992)

In spite of the uncertainties surrounding assessment, there was a very positive response among history teachers with regard to the view of history that underlies the NC. Teachers welcomed the emphasis on historical skills. However, once again, their enthusiasm for this aspect of the NC is diminished by the constraints that are the result of an overly prescribed content:

If you read through not just the final documents but all the interim reports along the way, there's been a major attempt by people involved in drawing up the document to state that they do recognize that the study of history involves a great range of activities on the part of pupils and a wide range of teaching methods. And that good learning and teaching in history comprises as wide a range of those methods as possible. And that's something that I absolutely agree with . . .

Certainly you can't understand history without knowing certain dates; it would be ludicrous to try and pretend that you could. But on the other hand, history isn't just a question of receiving information; [neither is it] just a question of going through processes and . . . different activities and assuming different skills. And I think the most rounded history course is one that involves a mixture of both. And I don't think the NC discourages that . . . all the interim reports along the way have made it perfectly clear that the people involved do recognize that history is more than just rote learning. But it is also more than just drama and information technology . . . And I think I perfectly agree with that . . . a good study of history involves learning what happens, but also learning why it happens.

However:

I think that there's simply a problem that the people who have drawn up this document have tended to say, 'well, in this topic' (maybe like 'Mediaeval Realms'), 'there are X number of things that are important,' without recognizing that the constraints on classroom teachers with the amount of contact time they have with classes, makes it very difficult to cover the content that they've prescribed in a way that teachers feel happy with . . .

I'm comfortable with it in principle. I'm rather less than comfortable with it in practice . . . So I think that really, it's a good idea, but it hasn't really been as well thought out as it could have been.

(HoD 3, 8 October 1992)

*Differences in teacher response*
When we consider differences between history teachers in their responses to the NC we find certain clear patterns. In this section we will explore some of the ways in which teachers' individual orientations and circumstances relate to their ways of responding to the NC.

A powerful theme that suffuses English and history teachers' views of effective teaching and learning, and which as we will show elsewhere in the book is of considerable concern to pupils too, is the role of affect in teaching and learning. All teachers recognize that pupil affect is important, though there is a range of views as to why this is. At one end of the spectrum pupil enjoyment of the subject is seen to be of paramount importance: 'it's always been very important to me that children, particularly little ones like this, enjoy their work' (Teacher 2, dept 2, 7 February 1992).

This teacher sees a major aim of the introductory year as being to enthuse pupils about the study of history, with the belief that pleasurable early experiences of the subject will provide an accumulation of good will towards the subject that can be drawn on in later years when the course demands are greater. For this teacher a major criterion for the selection of material should be accessibility and potential for stimulating pupil enjoyment and interest. These views form the basis for some of her objection to the forced pace of the curriculum (see above) and her reservations about its content. In the following example she is reflecting on the inclusion of study of the ancient Roman system of government:

> I think it's very complex. And I think I said before, if I didn't have the national curriculum to work through I'm not so sure that's something I would definitely include . . . I think I was maybe trying to get them to run before they could walk, you know. I mean, that sort of exercise – look at those sources and do this and this and this with them – is something that year 8, year 9 would just do.

Although in the second part of the quotation the teacher refers to the method by which the children were being taught the material, it is clear that this teacher (in common with the others in this study) sees her choice of method as being constrained by the content she is required to teach. This teacher is clear about how she feels this situation should be resolved: 'I feel that if anything's got to give, then I think the content of the National Curriculum's got to give.' Her concern here is that pupil engagement and understanding in lessons can sometimes be hampered by ineffective teaching, which she attributes, on the one hand, to inappropriate subject content and, on the other, to the demand to cover too much content in too brief a time. For her, one of the chief dangers of the NC is the way in which it may lead to a return to what she sees as traditional and unstimulating teaching methods:

> If I abandoned different classroom strategies and said, 'Right I've got this to do in this amount of time' . . . then I suppose, really, you'd be back to chalk and talk, and you'd be talking at them and they'd be writing and they'd do an odd picture. We'd be back to very, very old-fashioned, traditional methods, and they'd be bored stiff.

The head of department of teacher 2 shares her view that pupil affect is important as a motivator but responds slightly differently to the idea that there may be a conflict between the pupils' affective needs and the demands of the NC:

*I.* [Are you suggesting] that the NC might be forcing you to become more didactic in your teaching?

*HoD 2:* Occasionally, yes . . . but [generally] I . . . don't think so. No, I don't think it will [have that effect]. But I would be teaching like that if I felt it was necessary, wouldn't I, to get through the NC. No, I think that occasionally you may have to do your lessons like that just to fill in gaps and to move on to something that you think is perhaps more interesting to them, or more relevant or whatever.

For this head of department the NC is more of an accepted given than it is for her colleague. The principal task is to 'get through' the NC, and all else has to fit in behind this priority. Another point to bear in mind here is that this teacher is now talking with the benefit of hindsight, as she comes towards the end of the first year of the implementation of the NC in history. She is speaking from the confident viewpoint that the NC does not overly compromise her preferred teaching strategies. The message remains clear, however, that if it were to demand such a compromise, she would accept it.

This head of department is least critical, in a negative sense, of the NC, when compared to the other history teachers in the study. This is partly due to the fact that she has found the NC a rewarding experience in that it has helped her to revitalize her teaching: 'I think when you've been teaching a number of years, a jolt like this is very good. I'm very happy with it. I'm very pleased with the way it's all going really. And I feel I can see progress' (HoD 2, 10 April 1992). In this way, this teacher can be contrasted with the English teacher referred to earlier, who sees his own established ways of working as tried and tested and by virtue of this as bearing an authority that the NC does not possess.

The head of department 3 and his colleague are also concerned with pupil affect. Their concern, however, is expressed in slightly different terms from those used in department 2. They see 'fun' activities as providing 'light relief' for students, between less fun and more academic activities. 'If you've got some fun activities and then you have some less fun activities, and you go to fun activities, the variety will make them more amenable' (Teacher 5, dept 3, 5 November 1992). This view is underpinned by what might be termed a scholarly response to the NC, in that it is informed by an understanding of the nature of certain content items. For example, the nature of mediaeval farming is seen to be such that it has to be dealt with through the examination of fairly dry documents. This particular content does not lend itself (as one teacher sees it) to 'fun' and engaging activities such as role play or dramatic narrative. In this example, we can see how knowledge of subject and pedagogy combine to form what Shulman (1986) describes as 'pedagogical content knowledge', namely knowledge of the particular ways in which particular subject content knowledge is accessed.

Both of these teachers show an enthusiasm for the academic aspects of the NC, and indicate that they see the academic study of history as a central feature of their teaching. However, they also believe that the pupils they teach come from social backgrounds that do not prepare them well for academic study: hence the need for 'light relief'.

A further example of this 'scholarly' response to the NC is revealed in head of department 3's critical response to a particular aspect of NC content:

For example, in Mediaeval Realms, there's something that we're asked to do on the impact of Norman society across Western Europe, and that's immeasurable, I think really ... that you could spend a vast amount of time doing justice to that. And teachers, I think, are going to shy off from that because there aren't the resources and because teachers will see other things in the Norman Conquest as being of greater importance.

(HoD 3, 8 October 1992)

Here we can see how this teacher's way of thinking about operationalizing a particular curricular item is influenced by his own scholarly understanding of the content; that is, his own subject knowledge that has been developed through his own study of the subject.

Head of department 1, by contrast, has a rather prosaic reason for welcoming the NC, relating to internal 'school politics' and the demise of an integrated humanities curriculum in year 7, which combines history and geography in alternating modules taught by the same teachers: 'Yes, it's been good for me, cos I don't like this lower school humanities. National Curriculum history has been the *raison d'être* for getting rid of it. So it's an ally of mine, you see. So it's internal school politics' (HoD 1, June 1991). This is to be further contrasted with the concern expressed by members of department 2 that the NC will regrettably signal the demise of their Integrated Studies (IS) programme in year 7. They recognise that a flaw in the IS programme lies in the fact that individual teachers are required to deliver subjects (in their case English, geography and history) in which they are not specialists, with consequent patchiness in the quality of teaching. The NC is seen as demanding greater specialist subject knowledge (particularly in English and history). For them, however, what the IS programme lacks in academic rigour is compensated for by the social and affective benefits that their year 7 students accrue from developing the close relationship with the teacher who delivers all three subjects, and thus is a constant figure in their early experience of secondary school. Once again, this highlights something of the difficulty associated with meeting pupils' affective needs as a result of the NC.

### Individual differences

As with the English teachers, history teachers found little in the NC that they felt to be of benefit to children with learning difficulties. The sense, already expressed, that the weight of content and time constraints would lead to the superficial handling of certain content and leave less time than is necessary for detailed exploration was felt to be acute in relation to pupils with learning difficulties. Similarly, the potentially demoralizing effects of assigning pupils to lower levels than their peers were criticized.

The level of abstraction of certain content, as has already been noted, was felt to be excessive for year 7 pupils by some teachers; these teachers felt that pupils with learning difficulties would have their difficulties exacerbated by the inappropriateness of NC demands. On the other hand, one department (department 2) saw the need to provide all pupils with information that would enable them to chart their progress in NC terms:

> On our INSET day on Tuesday, [teacher 3] and I sat down and we've reworded all levels three to seven in what we think is language they'll understand. And next year our intention is to give every child a copy that they can keep in the back of their book, so if you award a level, and you're going through a piece of work, you can say, 'now look up what level this is and why you've achieved it, or you haven't.'
>
> (HoD 2, 8 March 1992)

This shows an overt intention at least to demystify the assessment process for all pupils.

### Effects on classroom practice

History teachers' perceptions of the effects of the NC on their classroom practice have already been illustrated to some degree. The reference in the previous section to the measures taken by the teachers in department 2 to give pupils knowledge of the assessment procedures is symptomatic of two major influences attributed to the NC by history teachers: (a) the influence of the NC on their planning and structuring of lessons, and (b) the influence of the NC in encouraging teachers to share the teaching–learning agenda with pupils.

With regard to the first of these, as has already been noted, history teachers planned their teaching entirely around the requirements of the NC, allocating specific lessons to the coverage of specific NC topics as defined in the Attainment Targets. According to these teachers the weight of content required a strict adherence to this lesson-by-lesson structure, which in turn led to an increase in pace of teaching and volume covered, when compared to pre-NC teaching. Furthermore, the demands of the NC led in certain cases to teachers covering material that was at a higher level of abstraction and difficulty than they would previously have attempted.

With regard to the second influence, history teachers, like many English teachers, attributed to the NC an increased, and in some cases new found, tendency to make explicit to pupils the learning objectives towards which they were working. This took the form of beginning lessons with recaps on previous lessons, and stating to pupils the learning agenda for the lesson, in terms of skills or statements of attainment to be addressed. This phenomenon is accounted for by teachers in terms of: their own greater clarity of precise learning objectives, in the form of historical skills and understanding as prescribed by the NC, which were being addressed in particular lessons; and their pragmatic need, for assessment purposes, to be able to account for pupil learning in NC terms. There was also repeated reference by history teachers to the increased emphasis on transmission styles in their teaching, which they attributed to the constraints imposed by the excessive content of the curriculum coupled with the limitations of time.

### Impact on departments

A major difference between the history and English departments in the current study is their relative size. English departments, for obvious reasons, tend usually to be among the largest departments in a school. The largest English department in the current study had 12 full-time or equivalent staff, while the smallest had 6.5. The largest history department had three full-time staff; the smallest had two full-time staff. Partly as a consequence of their smallness, the history departments tended to have more effective channels of communication among the members, facilitated by the opportunities that a small group of people have for regular informal contact. Issues that English departments would have to deal with in formally called departmental meetings, that ensured the presence of all members, could be handled in passing when members of the history department came together in non-contact and break times. Consequently, the NC was perceived to have less of an impact on the formal organization of history departments. Like the English departments, however, the NC was seen to have a considerable effect on the degree of standardization and coordination of teaching throughout the departments. As in English, history departments produced modular plans which prescribed for each teacher the particular aspects of the NC that were to be covered at a given time. Therefore, as in English, idiosyncrasy and individuality in the choice of curriculum content virtually disappeared in history (though such curricular idiosyncrasy was not seen to be as rife as it appears to have been in English departments prior to the NC, and was not considered by history teachers to be a particularly significant issue).

### Conclusion

In the light of some of the key theoretical issues raised in Chapter 1, it is clear that the predominant orientation among both English and history teachers is (to refer back to Ball and Bowe's typology) an 'interpretation' as opposed to 'implementation' response to the NC. Our analysis does, however, show that the simple opposition between implementation and interpretation does not capture fully the complexity of the detailed responses of the teachers in our study.

The detailed analysis reveals some individual differences in the degree to which teachers are prepared to challenge and deviate from the dictates of the NC. The common thread here is teachers' implicit view of themselves as active participants in the construction of the curriculum as it is taught. Their contribution to this process draws on their professional and scholarly knowledge about effective ways of teaching and pupils' learning needs, as well as, in some cases, the knowledge they have derived as scholars in their teaching subjects. There is an ongoing, though sometimes understated, sense of tension between teachers' view of themselves as active and critical professionals/scholars and the prescriptive qualities of the NC. This conflict is most active in English in relation to the assessment components of the NC, while in history the conflict focuses on the weight of curriculum content. In both these cases teachers complain of the failure of the curriculum designers to take sufficient account of knowledge that teachers themselves consider to be central to practical curriculum development. There are also important variations in response which suggest ways in which the individual teacher's response can be influenced by the departmental context.

In summary, the complex and subtle patterns identified in teachers' responses to the NC can be expressed in terms of the following issues:

- the wide diversity of reasons the teachers give for welcoming and engaging constructively with the NC;
- the different interpretations of the NC that teachers adopt in order to accommodate its demands without compromising their pedagogical values;
- variations in response that can be associated with different subject cultures, and between different ideological positions within the same subject area;
- variations in response that can be related to teachers' perceptions of the nature and range of the individual differences they perceive between pupils;
- the complex relationship between individual and departmental responses;
- occasional conflict between the perceived effects of the NC on teachers' practice, and the apparent effects, as judged from teachers' own accounts;
- the felt need to comply with certain aspects of the NC while maintaining severe mental reservations about its validity;
- the critical and selective approach to the NC of some teachers, which allows them to comply with some aspects of the NC while rejecting other aspects;
- the significance of the temporal context (time scale considerations), which influences teachers' response to the NC in terms of their short- and long-term concerns in relation to pupil learning.

# 4/ *Teachers' craft knowledge*

In this chapter we take a close look at some of the knowledge that under-pins what teachers see as successful classroom teaching. We refer to this area of knowledge and understanding as teachers' professional craft knowledge (Desforges and McNamara 1979; Brown and McIntyre 1993). We are concerned with the nature of this knowledge and how teachers use it on a day-to-day basis.

This part of our study grew directly out of an earlier study carried out by Brown and McIntyre (1993). It is, therefore, appropriate to consider our present findings in the light of this earlier work. In particular, we wish to explore the extent to which the current findings support or challenge the generalizability of the conclusions drawn from the earlier work. This is of particular interest when we consider the differences in the two research contexts, which are marked by the fact that the first study was carried out in Scotland as opposed to England, as well as the fact that the second study was carried out at a time when the National Curriculum was a new or relatively new feature of the working context. A further distinction to be drawn between the two studies concerns the fact that while the first study was concerned with teachers' and pupils' perceptions of effective teaching, in its broadest sense, the current study is primarily concerned with perceptions of teaching that is deemed to be effective in terms of pupil learning. The second study, therefore, should be seen as part rep-lication and part extension of the original study.

Before we develop these points, however, it is necessary to say something about some of the assumptions that underpin this aspect of our research.

## The nature of professional craft knowledge

Professional craft knowledge – as opposed to other forms of knowledge that teachers might possess – is the knowledge that experienced teachers gather throughout their careers that enables them to make decisions about how best to approach professional tasks. This knowledge is firmly rooted in teachers' practical experience, and is directly linked to their daily practice. By definition, craft knowledge describes the knowledge that arises from and, in turn, informs what teachers actually do. As such, this knowledge is to be distinguished from other forms of knowledge that are not linked to practice in this direct way. Craft knowledge is not, therefore, the kind of knowledge that teachers draw on when explaining the thinking underlying their ideal teaching practices. Neither is it knowledge drawn from theoretical sources. Professional craft knowledge can certainly be (and often is) informed by these sources, but it is of a far more practical nature than these knowledge forms. Professional craft knowledge is the knowledge that teachers develop through the processes of reflection and practical problem-solving that they engage in to carry out the demands of their jobs. As such this knowledge is informed by each teacher's individual way of thinking and knowing.

A problem here is that while experienced teachers clearly possess such knowledge, the culture of teaching and the nature of schools are such that this knowledge is often not articulated. The working lives of teachers are dominated by the demand to perform effectively, with precious little space for reflection and consultation with colleagues. The time that teachers do have for reflection and development outside the classroom is often insufficient for the kind of exploration that the uncovering of craft knowledge requires. The experience of the present study, however, shows us clearly that teachers place a high value on the opportunity to articulate this knowledge, and it is suggested that the process of articulation enables teachers to obtain deeper understandings of their own practice than would be possible without such articulation.

Because of the often tacit nature of professional craft knowledge, it is difficult to access. In Chapter 2 we dealt with the special measures we took in order to maximize our trust in the authenticity of the findings presented here.

## Teachers' professional craft knowledge: conclusions from the Scottish study

Brown and McIntyre's original study of 16 Scottish teachers (12 secondary and four primary) and their pupils produced an account of the ways in which teachers construed effective teaching in its broadest sense. On the basis of this study, Brown and MacIntyre came to the following conclusions.

1  In the first instance teachers without exception evaluated the merits of their teaching in practice with reference to pupil outcomes. Thus,

when asked to talk about what had gone well in lessons, all the teachers first spoke not in terms of their own performance, but in terms of what the pupils had been doing and what the pupils had achieved.

2 Only with some difficulty were teachers in general able to go on to articulate what they had done to achieve such desirable outcomes.

3 The kinds of pupil outcomes referred to by teachers tended to be short term. Teachers hardly ever spontaneously included any reference to ways in which these short-term outcomes might contribute to longer-term benefits.

4 The most common type of outcomes referred to by teachers were 'normal desirable states of classroom activity' (NDSs). NDSs were defined in terms of pupil behaviour that teachers perceived to be desirable because it was deemed appropriate to various prevalent classroom conditions, including the nature of the task and the phase of the lesson.

5 A second less common type of desirable outcome was that of pupil 'progress'. Three types of progress were identified in relation to observable developments in: (a) pupils' knowledge, understanding or skills; (b) the completion of a product, such as an artefact or completed exercise; and (c) completion of a set of tasks or coverage of a particular content area.

6 Relatively few of the outcomes were explicitly concerned with curriculum learning goals.

7 Teachers seemed to have an extensive repertoire of possible actions from which to draw in order to bring about the more limited range of outcomes with which they were commonly concerned. Actions included: teacher modelling of desired pupil behaviour; use of story to stimulate empathy for a historical figure; specific presentational styles and strategies.

8 Teachers drew on these repertoires in ways that took account of a multiplicity of factors of many kinds which they saw as relevant to their particular situations. These included specific aspects of the physical environment, pupil characteristics, time constraints, lesson content, teaching materials and the teacher's own emotional state and habits of behaviour.

9 When evaluating the outcomes they observed, teachers took account of a similar range of conditions to those referred to above (8).

10 Most prominent among the factors of which teachers took account were those relating to pupil characteristics. These included immediate behavioural and performance characteristics, as well as more enduring perceived qualities of individual children, such as their ability and motivation levels, and aspects of pupil temperament.

11 Teachers were frequently faced with a need to attain more than one outcome at the same time, and frequently this was important in determining the course taken.

12 Where teachers' craft knowledge was inadequate to cope with the multiple outcomes required, teachers would generally act to achieve those outcomes that they considered to be of highest priority.

## Elements of teachers' craft knowledge identified in the present study

When we approached teachers in the current study and asked them to talk about effective aspects of their teaching we found some strong resonances with Brown and McIntyre's work, as well as some interesting points of difference, which we will expand on. First, as in the Scottish study, we found that teachers' concerns with effective pupil learning are located among an array of other concerns about the need to manage the teaching and learning context, and that teachers' ideas about what it means to be an effective teacher encompass the full range of concerns among which pupil learning outcomes are but one. As will be seen in the following chapter, these wider concerns are very important in distinguishing teachers' thinking from that of pupils. In this chapter, however, emphasis will be given to the aspect of teachers' craft knowledge that contributes to effective pupil learning, as perceived by teachers.

Four major dimensions were used by teachers in this study to make judgements about the effectiveness of their teaching. These dimensions were:

- their long-term *aims*, in relation to pupil outcomes over an extended time scale (such as a term, year or pupils' school careers), and their professional commitments (e.g. 'coverage' of syllabus);
- their short-term *objectives*, in relation to pupil outcomes and progress, over a narrow time scale (such as a lesson, group of lessons or half-termly 'unit');
- their own *performance*, in terms of decisions made in preactive and/or interactive phases of lessons, their management and presentational skills, and the success and appropriateness of their teaching methods;
- their preferred *image*, in relation to the type of classroom state they seek to maintain, through the promotion of particular forms of interaction (social and interpersonal) and pupil behaviour.

Immediately, it is interesting to note some divergence from the findings of the Scottish study. The concerns with long-term aims contrasts strongly with the emphasis on pupil outcomes that Brown and McIntyre identified. Similarly, teachers in the present study were keen and able to talk in considerable detail about their own performance, and its relationship to learning outcomes, in ways that teachers in the Scottish study seemed to find more difficult. The current teachers' concerns with short-term objectives do seem to correspond well with the Scottish teachers' concerns with pupil outcomes, NDSs and issues of progress. The concept of 'image' is also a feature of our findings that is not present in the Brown and McIntyre study. The suggestion here is that the images used by teachers when thinking about their craft are not simply a means of communicating their understandings; rather, the images actually shape the content of the knowledge.

These points of convergence and divergence between the present study and the study by Brown and McIntyre will be developed in the following elaboration of the four dimensions outlined above.

## Teachers' aims

When teachers talked about their aims for a given lesson or unit, both preactively and retrospectively, they often referred to one or both of two categories of aims: 'affective' aims and 'cognitive' aims. These categories emerge as important to teachers because they were often presented in terms that suggest the difficulties inherent in attempting to address what they perceived to be qualitatively different types of aims simultaneously. Like the teachers in the Scottish study, the teachers in the current study found competing aims sometimes mutually inconsistent. Affective and cognitive aims were often cited as representing such an opposition. Teachers often believed they had to choose between affective and cognitive aims or prioritize one type of aim over the other, because their craft knowledge did not enable them to meet both aims simultaneously.

Prominent affective aims include engendering in pupils a sense of security and willingness to participate in class/group discussion, and encouraging pupils to adopt a positive attitude to the subject area and to derive pleasure from study. Ms Brown, an English teacher, illustrates the use of affective aims: 'I'm looking particularly, I suppose, at imaginative writing . . . and I want to teach them that English is interesting and dynamic, that it's got so many off-shoots – so many facets you can explore . . . And also just to enjoy it.' Notable here is the prominence of affective aims relating to pupil interest and enjoyment, and the relative vagueness, signalled by the teacher's uncertainty, in relation to cognitive, subject focused goals.

Cognitive aims related to pupils' acquisition of particular knowledge, their cognitive development, their understanding of concepts and their mastery of specific skills, as is demonstrated in the following extract.

One of the main aims which I want to try and address this week is: what is particularly special to the dramatic form as opposed to the novel for example? Why should writers choose to write in a dramatic form rather than in prose? And also I think it's important to address that question with the children and say, 'What's actually the difference

between drama and prose?' The reason being, it seems to me that . . .
when they come to GCSE the exam boards require the students to
write on plays, but the questions are nearly always content based . . . very
rarely does an examination question focus on the actual form of
writing. That's a thing that I think is very important, actually.

In this case the teacher's rationale was closely related to his own view of
his subject and the type of knowledge that he believed it necessary for
pupils to have. This teacher made no reference at all during this interview
to any affective aims he might have had for his pupils. Elsewhere, he
revealed that the importance of affective aims lay for him, primarily, in
the degree to which they contributed to the achievement of cognitive
goals. For this teacher, then, cognitive goals invariably took precedence
over affective goals.

Although the emphasis on cognitive and affective domains carried across
both history and English subject areas, there are important distinctions to
be made which relate to subject differences. Because the National Curriculum in history was perceived by teachers in this study to be more
highly prescriptive in terms of content and learning outcomes than the
English curriculum, history teachers had a tendency to centre their descriptions of their aims around learning objectives. However, among the
history teachers it is possible to distinguish between the majority of teachers
who prioritized cognitive over affective aims, and the one teacher who
consistently emphasized the primacy of affective concerns. This is illustrated by comparing the accounts of two teachers, the first of which places
a high value on pupil understanding and the second of which is prepared
to sacrifice understanding in favour of meeting what she sees as pupils'
affective needs: 'I'm feeling under pressure about getting through it all . . . I
do actually believe in explaining to them the coherence of the course. So
I wanted to make it clear that we are now moving to look at problems with
government.' The second teacher made the following statement, having
just described the way in which she had curtailed an exposition in order
to prevent the pupils from becoming bored:

> I'm very wary about going on [to pupils] about it [i.e. the national
> curriculum attainment targets] because . . . the most important thing
> to me in this is that they're enjoying it. . . . If I start going on about
> [it] they'll all switch off. I don't want them to do that because I don't
> want them to think that history's got to be laboured.

In contrast to other history teachers this teacher expressed a degree of
uncertainty about the extent to which she needed to make learning targets explicit to pupils: 'I don't know how much to go on about it [i.e.
attainment targets]. That's something else that I'm puzzled about at the
moment: whether or not to tell them about what we did.'

One history department managed this dilemma by planning its teaching from National Curriculum programmes of study in terms of 'heavy' and 'light relief' tasks. 'Heavy' tasks were rendered 'heavy' by the cognitive difficulties posed by their subject matter for the majority of year 7 pupils. 'Light relief' topics were cognitively less demanding and were chosen with a strong emphasis on the likely enjoyment that pupils would derive from them. The aim was to create a balance between heavy and light relief activities. So, for example, the topic of the Roman system of government was considered to be a 'heavy' topic, because the most effective means these teachers identified for teaching the topic involved a considerable amount of fairly dry text-based work. Furthermore, they considered the concepts that pupils were required to understand to be of little likely intrinsic interest to their year 7 pupils. In order to balance this affectively unrewarding topic, they ensured at the planning stage that this topic would be followed by the study of the growth of the Roman Empire. This topic afforded 'light relief' because it was believed to be conceptually straightforward and rendered 'concrete' by the use of maps. It was also made attractive by the availability of 'The Roman Empire Game', which was a resource-based activity designed to engage pupils in learning through play. In this way the teachers attempted to meet the rigour required by the National Curriculum (cognitive aims), as well as what they saw as his pupils' need for affective relief.

This primary concern with relatively long-term aims contrasts with the short-term concerns that were the chief focus of teachers in the Scottish study. There are two possible reasons for this apparent inconsistency, the first methodological and the second substantive.

First, in the Scottish study the teachers were asked by the researchers to talk about any aspect of their teaching that they believed to have 'gone well'. The more restricted focus of the present study on teaching that led to effective learning may account for the differences in response, given that the current group of teachers displayed concern for a similar range of pupil outcomes to that shown by the Scottish teachers, when they were able to speak in more general terms about their teaching.

Second, the National Curriculum, as was noted in Chapter 3, was a major source of concern to the teachers in this study because of the unique historical circumstances that meant that the research was being carried out as teachers grappled with the NC for the first time. A particular feature of the NC is its focus on long-term aims, and, as we saw in Chapter 3, this was experienced as something of a departure from habit for a number of teachers, many of whom indicated that their pre-NC thinking had been less informed by long-term concerns. This is not to say that the long-term thinking identified here was necessarily explicitly NC specific; what is explicit is the practice of thinking in broader time scales and long-term outcomes. This finding may, therefore, indicate further ways in which the NC influenced teachers' ways of thinking about their teaching. The degree to which such influence is sustained is a question that must be addressed by further research. It is possible, of course, that what is being identified here is simply the immediate response to a novel situation.

The particular preoccupation with two major types of aims, the cognitive and affective, may also be accounted for in relation to these issues. The NC, as Chapter 3 indicates, was seen by teachers in this study very much as an abstraction from the teaching and learning process, in that it draws out content issues and fails to account for the ways in which content and pedagogy are necessarily interrelated in the minds of professional teachers. This abstraction of 'content' can itself be seen as placing an emphasis on the cognitive aspects of education and learning that the teachers in the Scottish study were not exposed to.

**Teachers' objectives**

The term 'objectives' refers to teachers' talk about their short-term plans for and outcomes of individual lessons and units. This corresponds very closely with findings from the Scottish study, which showed how teachers focused on this aspect of their teaching. In the present study, teachers described these short-term concerns primarily in terms of cognitive and affective objectives relating to observed pupil outcomes. Cognitive objectives are characterized by an orientation towards instrumental outcomes, while affective objectives tend to centre on 'expressive' concerns (Eisner 1985).

Cognitive objectives are often expressed in terms of pupils' skilled performance in intellectual tasks that are of a cross-curricular nature (e.g. articulating responses to teacher inputs, evaluation and interpretation), the state of their subject knowledge (e.g. factual recall, procedural knowledge), and their mastery of subject-related skills (e.g. character study in English; recognizing bias in an historical source). Here an English teacher cited pupils' ability to ask apposite questions relating to literary forms as an important objective:

> I certainly think that my immediate objectives over the five or six lessons have been addressed, and I'm fairly satisfied that I've hit the majority of children with that, regardless of difference in ability, in terms of encouraging them to ask questions on the form rather than just merely the content of what they've been reading . . . I'm quite pleased to hear them thinking in fairly sophisticated way for year 7 kids about the actual form of the thing.

Affective objectives and outcomes were often expressed, by both history and English teachers, in terms of pupil enjoyment and enthusiasm for tasks and subjects: 'I want them to get the idea of concentrating and also enjoy doing it.' 'Basically we were having fun playing with words and drawing silly pictures, with the . . . implication of something more serious.'

## Normal desirable states of pupil activity

As in the Scottish study, it is useful to employ the concept of normal desirable states (NDSs) (Brown and McIntyre 1993) here, to refer to the tendency among teachers to talk about individual lessons in terms of the types of pupil activity they sought to maintain. These NDSs, at different times, reflected different concerns, which can be discussed in terms of technical and affective objectives. Typical technical NDSs related to evidence of pupil engagement with the learning content of the lesson, such as their performance in answering questions, the types of questions they asked or the evidence of cooperation and understanding shown in group discussion. Affective NDSs were more often concerned with the quality of social inter-action in the classroom and evidence of emotional states. Descriptions of positive affective and cognitive outcomes were often framed in terms of lessons having 'gone well'. A lesson was seen to have gone well affectively when pupils appeared to show that they had enjoyed the lesson, or appeared to have worked harmoniously together: 'I was fairly happy that they were all busy and that nobody was bored because they didn't understand anything, and nobody was bored because they'd done everything too quickly or anything like that.' Where teachers talked in terms of lessons having gone well from a cognitive point of view, they tended to cite evidence of conceptual development or other signs of cognitive performance:

You've got to remember that at this time of term they're tired as well – I've noticed that – slacking off of concentration and effort. [But] no they weren't bad, they're still making the connections [i.e. showing evidence of recognition of common themes across different historical periods and topics] that I was pleased about last term.

Sometimes affective NDSs were cited as contributing to the achievement of particular cognitive outcomes. In this case, pupil 'interest' (i.e. affective NDS) was seen to contribute to the lesson by motivating 'weaker' pupils to contribute 'useful' information to the lesson:

[I was pleased with] the general level of involvement and interest [of pupils in the lesson]. I think that the weaker members of the group: their ideas were good; they perhaps didn't express them so well on paper, but they certainly came up with some useful ideas . . . I think I got over the message, at the end, that history is based on evidence, and we need to have theories, but we need evidence to back up our theories.

An important sub-group of NDSs related to teachers concern with pupils conduct. An example of this was provided by an English teacher reflecting on her organization of classroom groups: 'I'd deliberately built groups of four, so there weren't too many children sitting round saying, "I don't know what to do. I'll go and wander round and see what's going on in the classroom."' A second English teacher exemplified a disciplinary NDS: 'I come down very heavily on the sniggers. This morning it was happening when he [a pupil] talked about ... he slipped, because he was aware he was in centre stage ... So, therefore, I picked that up: "this is nasty; you're [the class] being silly to laugh at him."' This example also shows how the teacher's disciplinary intervention had the effect of supporting an affective NDS.

## Teacher performance

A striking point of contrast between the findings of the current study and those of the Scottish study is the way in which teachers in the present study talked about their performance. While Brown and McIntyre found that the teachers they studied made few spontaneous references to their own performance in relation to successful classroom teaching, and had difficulty in talking about this when asked, in the current study teachers often appeared at ease in talking about the success and appropriateness of their teaching methods, as well as being forthcoming and articulate on this subject.

When reflecting on their own performance during lessons teachers emphasized two different aspects of their classroom behaviour. They tended, on the one hand, to talk about the ways in which their performance related to the learning aims that they had established in the preactive phase and, on the other, to talk more in terms of the ways in which they responded or reacted to prevalent conditions during the interactive phase of lessons. As in the Scottish study, the conditions of which teachers took account were many and various, but the largest category of them was of pupil characteristics.

An English teacher gave an example of her effective presentation of material to pupils, which also showed the value she attached to the quality of teacher–pupil interaction:

> I think probably, reading that little piece of work [reading a student's essay aloud to the class] was quite effective, because I don't think they were expecting that. I think it was also effective, my standing there and asking if I may [i.e. getting student's permission] ... Because it was his [essay] ... I would have liked to have read the whole script [aloud] but I didn't want to, you know, bare his inner soul.

This is another example of the delicacy with which these teachers treated students' affective needs. Here the teacher was prepared to sacrifice what she believes would have been a cognitively valuable experience for the whole class (i.e. being exposed to a good model of essay writing) in favour of a student's 'finer feelings'.

Teachers were also sometimes concerned with their self-presentation in a more general sense. In the following example an English teacher referred to the kind of persona she wished to present to her pupils: 'I think you have to [be charismatic], certainly my colleagues always seem to be very charismatic as well. You've got to come in, when you're feeling like death, and virtually perform on occasion.'

Teachers' modes of self-presentation were often closely related to the particular objectives they had for lessons. For example, the same teacher carried on from her comments about charisma to say: 'today, socially and organizationally, these children have got to learn that it isn't acceptable not to do your homework . . . So the guise of being very angry had to be put on, as I walked through the door.' On a further occasion, this teacher explained how she used self-projection techniques to demonstrate the nature of a Shakespearean character, thus indicating how this aspect of teacher performance can be used for the achievement of cognitive objectives.

A history teacher provided an example of how teachers related their performance to pupil learning outcomes: 'I was quite surprised . . . about the connections they did make between the understanding and the activity. I mean, obviously I'd set it up by putting that on the board.' This also represents a model of teacher effect. This model was exemplified elsewhere, when an English teacher gave an example of the extent to which her performance was goal-related:

> Sometimes I have a conscience that when you do things like this [i.e. groupwork with a 'scribe'] . . . some children are getting away with not doing any writing, and those children are usually . . . the ones who should be doing the writing. So I think I would actually say, 'I want you *all* to write down the instructions [related to the set group task] . . . You all write down the instructions so you've got a copy of it. So that some of them are just practising writing more than anything.

When teachers talked about their performance in terms of decision-making, they often referred to the *appropriateness* of their choice of tasks. In this case 'appropriateness' is considered in relation to issues of individual differences among pupils:

> In terms of differences among pupils . . . I generally sat down and thought, 'Probably it's more – this is a . . . middle approach, to see what the brighter ones make of it and what the weaker ones make of

it' . . . There are times . . . when I . . . say, 'This is a bit weak for the bottom end, and it's not necessarily stretching the brighter ones.'

In the following quotation the same teacher describes her sense of satisfaction with the range of material she had provided for pupils as models for the writing of autobiographies. Once again, her particular concern was with the issue of individual differences among pupils:

> I thought there was a good range in that material in that some of it's very simple, and they can imitate it. So like with Jim [pupil with learning difficulties], with the 'I wish' poem, I was very pleased cos he can copy most of it and add some. And Jim is literally at that stage really, where [it is] very hard [for him] to write freely. But to actually copy, and then add an idea – so I thought it was good to range from that [low level] through to 'Salford Road' [poem], which is slightly obscure and retrospective.

In suggesting possible reasons for the unexpected emphasis that these teachers placed on their own performance characteristics, in contrast to the teachers in the Scottish study, it seems appropriate to refer to a number of issues:

- as Chapter 3 suggested, the advent of the NC appears to have encouraged many of the teachers in this study to engage in reflection and talk with colleagues about effective teaching methods;
- the NC, quite clearly, made teachers conscious of their responsibility for facilitating pupil progress through the NC attainment targets and key stages;
- the different research methods used, which encouraged teachers to talk more discursively, and led them in particular to talk about their pre-lesson planning, may have led them to talk more about their own performance than did the Scottish focus on 'What went well?'

## Teachers' classroom images

Teachers' reports of their practice often contained references to their preferred 'images' (Elbaz 1981, 1983; Clandinin 1986). Classroom 'images' are defined as 'brief descriptive and sometimes metaphoric statements' (Elbaz 1983: 254) that are made by teachers in order to communicate aspects of their craft knowledge. Images function as frameworks within which teachers structure and process their classroom experience. They are generated from the interaction between teachers' experience of teaching and their broader field of personal experience, and are characterized by strong emotional and moral associations which root them deeply in teachers' thought processes (Clandinin 1986). The particular images employed by a teacher can therefore provide the researcher with insight into the constraints and opportunities that the teacher perceives, since the image is both a product of such perceptions and a means by which these are maintained. Images are not only ways of framing these constraints and opportunities; their nature is actually to *delimit* them. Images become, therefore, an integral part of craft knowledge.

This use by teachers of distinctive individual imagery is highly consistent with the Scottish finding that teachers' craft knowledge was characterized by individually distinctive criteria for normal desirable states of activity and equally individual repertoires of pedagogical actions. That the imagery itself is more marked in the present study is perhaps a reflection of the greater opportunities given to teachers to talk more discursively about their teaching.

This study provided examples of teachers' images of:

- self;
- their teaching subjects;
- their pupils;
- the teaching process;
- the classroom environment.

Teachers employed images to elucidate areas of their classroom teaching, but not always to draw attention to desirable features. In this extract we find an English teacher giving an account of her teaching style, and in so doing showing how by virtue of her personal biography she holds conflicting beliefs which influence her classroom practice in sometimes negative ways:

> I've always thought that you should do that [i.e. be a transmitter of knowledge to pupils]. I was brought up by parents who were wonderful but they always told me [what to do], and I'm rather guilty of that [in the classroom] at times, I think. I'm a sort of fairly 'housewifey' sort of teacher, I think. I'm very sort of fundamental and basic . . . And I think it's very dangerous. I mean, I think they've got to be free to find their own interpretation of things; bring their own response to things and to give what they've got.

In the following two examples we see how a teacher's classroom images appear to have influenced her practice:

> As soon as I betray a trust then I've lost [teacher as leader] them, haven't I? I think . . . stopping and questioning en route [lesson as journey] . . . you have to do it. I think that's effective, and if you don't do it then you don't know quite who's following you at all [teacher as leader and lesson as journey] . . . I've always been on red alert [military/conflict/battle]. It's the teacher with experience being on

red alert to see who's always giving information. And obviously at the moment, they are secure and they are happy and they're OK.

I think very carefully before I come in . . . these children have got to learn that it isn't acceptable not to do your homework. And so the guise of being very angry had to be put on as I walked through the door. And that was just walking straight right, centre stage, and leaning on the table waiting for them. I didn't say a thing. It was all charade [teacher as actor].

These extracts reveal a view of pupils as being manipulated and 'led' by the teacher. The teacher's role here moves between that of leader, soldier and actor, with the students fulfilling the corresponding roles of tourists, the enemy and audience.

Other teachers defined pupils in more dynamic terms, seeing them, for example, as possessors of tacit knowledge. Where teachers expressed this view of pupils they described their own role as facilitating pupil articulation of tacit knowledge, as opposed to 'leading'. In the following example the teacher was talking in terms of giving emphasis to particular subject knowledge, and providing a 'framework' in which pupils could apply their tacit knowledge:

Well, I'm pleased with the way that, through their talk, they seem to be using their own implicit knowledge about language to make their own statements, and, therefore, taking it a step further in their own learning. And that's not coming from me a lot of the time. Because I do believe that all children have a strong implicit knowledge of language that the teacher needs to tease out, or to set up lessons that will enable the students to verbalize that; to bring it out themselves . . . I've tried to give them some framework about what I perceive to be the important pointers about how language works and how language changes . . . what I try to do is just give them apposite examples of that, and again, we try to make that interesting, we try and make that humorous, in the hope that that will be sparking off thoughts in their own mind. So I mean I could stand at the board and give them notes, and they could copy. But [instead] through a series of examples, and through that framework, actually asking them to try and make more of the links themselves.

This extract shows how this teacher's images of the subject matter, his students and his role as teacher intertwined and interacted. The particular importance of his view of students' constructive abilities is emphasized by his preference for the student-centred approach he seems, by his own claims, to have adopted. This was a consistent feature of this teacher's teaching, as was demonstrated on a different occasion with entirely different subject matter:

Today we're going to have a short session. So I would just like to frame that question ['How is it different if a writer chooses to tell a story using a play as opposed to a novel?']; introduce it to them. And in pair and group work I'm going to be asking them to brainstorm some ideas themselves. But it seems to me that it's important to use the children's own, if you like, repertoire of reading, or their own skills, to try and answer those questions. I mean, it would be quite easy for me to stand at the front [of the class] and tell them what I think the difference is, but that would be a nonsense. So we're going to start off by just asking them to think in groups about that question and brainstorm some ideas and put them on the board, to have a discussion lesson based on that today.

Some images had a more pervasive quality than others, as was demonstrated by a history teacher when she indicated the relationship between a particular personal image and key aims she saw herself as pursuing in her teaching:

I can remember when I was at school [as a pupil], a lot of teachers would just stand at the front of the classroom and it would be . . . and you'd sit there thinking, 'Oh,' you know, 'I wonder what I could do at break?' You wouldn't be listening, and you wouldn't be actively involved in your learning. And I think it does help – even little things like they did today, the dialogue between the two of you from a script – it boosts confidence . . . I would like to think that, when children come out my classrooms, they actually think: 'I've learnt something today,' or, 'I enjoyed that.' Because when I think back to my own days at school, there was many a lesson I walked out of and I just thought, 'That was hard work!' or, you know, '[We've] got so and so now, and that will be just as bad.' I suppose it's me not wanting to be like people who taught me in some respects.

The central image here is of the teacher's own experience of being a bored and sometimes bewildered school student. This image is then related with her own central preoccupation with making learning purposeful and enjoyable for pupils: a preoccupation that was borne out in other interviews. Her particular concern was to avoid being like her former teachers. This intention was enacted in her repeated conscious avoidance of lengthy oral explanations in the classroom, and her willingness to allow lessons to be shaped on occasions by students' interests rather than the particular learning outcomes she has pre-planned. This image was also reflected in her own repeated claim to require variety and stimulation in her teaching. This example illustrates the way in which a teacher's imagery had a profound influence on the kinds of decisions that she made about appropriate aims and methods in teaching. In this case key personal imagery highlights the areas of teacher performance that are of particular significance.

## The importance of cognitive and affective considerations

It should be clear by now that both cognitive and affective considerations were important for the teachers in the present study. Affective considerations deal with the establishment of a particular social climate in the classroom. Cognitive considerations tend to focus on aspects of the formal curriculum. Craft knowledge is informed by both cognitive and affective considerations, along with other factors. Affective concerns feed into teachers' craft knowledge in the form of understandings and beliefs about students' emotionality and the dynamics of interpersonal and social interaction. Cognitive issues inform craft knowledge through the medium of subject knowledge, and understandings about how children learn, as well as knowledge of appropriate teaching methods. These considerations form continuous strands throughout the teachers' accounts of their craft knowledge. It is important to note the different ways in which they interacted with one another. Sometimes they could be seen to take the form of competing concerns, while at other times they intertwined and operated in ways that were complementary. On yet other occasions affective and cognitive concerns were addressed separately. The ways in which these concerns related to one another were a constant preoccupation for these teachers as will be shown in the following sections.

The earlier consideration of the role of imagery highlights individual and idiosyncratic aspects of teachers' craft knowledge. It highlights the ways in which teachers' thinking about their craft can be wrapped up with their very personal life experience. And this alerts us to the bewildering variety of teaching styles and types that are possible. One of the interesting things here, however, is not the wide diversity of imagery used by teachers but the commonalities in the concerns that were the focus of their imagery.

The examples above illustrate a continuing preoccupation among the teachers with issues of teacher control and student involvement. All these teachers, even the one espousing the least dynamic image of her students, were concerned with creating a situation in their classrooms that not only enabled them to perform as effective teachers, but also enabled their students to perform as active learners. The important issue here is that the teachers all recognized that effective learning is not necessarily associated with effective teaching in a linear sense. On the one hand, teachers were concerned with their performance as instructors and expositors of knowledge, and often talked at length about their performance in this area.

They were concerned, for example, with the appositeness of the examples they used when illustrating a point, or their use of diagrams, or the ways in which they employed students' explanations to get the teaching point across. On the other hand, however, there were times when they claimed to have contributed very little to the positive learning outcomes that they observed in their lessons. A typical comment supporting this point was: 'I was very pleased with the way in which they brought those different ideas together in this lesson. Though I don't think it had anything to do with me – they did it all.' What is interesting about this often repeated scenario is that the teachers seemed to express the same satisfaction in these circumstances as they did when they believed the learning outcomes to be directly associated with their teaching. Teachers' major preoccupations were with the outcomes of lessons, rather than the means by which the outcomes were achieved. We will deal in a little more detail with the nature of the outcomes sought by teachers later. At the moment it is sufficient to emphasize that for these teachers evidence of successful student outcomes was at least as great (and sometimes greater) a source of satisfaction as evidence of particularly effective teaching. This observation is consistent with the findings of Brown and McIntyre, in their Scottish study, and once again underlines the influence of the researchers' focus on the research findings of the two studies.

The strong indication, illustrated above, that teachers were highly goal-oriented in their thinking about their teaching craft would seem to be related to their concern with student involvement and teacher control of the classroom environment and learning agenda. These teachers were concerned to achieve certain outcomes in their classrooms, which, as we will see, related in different ways to their students' learning. Some of the outcomes sought by teachers might more accurately be termed 'processes' or 'conditions' (such as forms of student interaction or individual behaviour, classroom ethos or social climate), and these often relate to the affective realm, rather than the cognitive, in that they represent a concern with the need to create circumstances in the classroom that are conducive to certain states of student feeling or orientation, which in turn help to motivate students to engage actively in the learning process as individuals and cooperate with other students and the teacher.

## Conclusion

This chapter has described and illustrated some of the key features of the craft knowledge of the teachers in this study. We have shown some of the key ways in which these teachers thought about episodes of effective teaching. In doing this we have also shown some of the ways in which findings of the present study can be related to the earlier study of teachers' craft knowledge that was carried out by Brown and McIntyre (1993) in Scotland. Taken together the two studies illustrate the complexity of the thought processes that underpin skilled teaching. In particular, the studies show how teachers draw on a vast array of knowledge of specific data in making pedagogical decisions, and in assessing teaching priorities.

A key finding of Brown and McIntyre's original study was concerned with the ways in which teachers took considerable account of particular contextual information in their thinking and decision-making. It is not surprising, therefore, that some of the differences between the findings of the two studies can also be considered in relation to contextual differences. In particular, the advent of the National Curriculum would appear to have encouraged the teachers in the current study to be more reflective about their own influence on the learning process, and to be more concerned with their own performance as teachers than the teachers in the earlier study. Their greater degree of expansiveness on these issues may also account for the apparently greater significance of teachers' use of personal imagery in their accounts of their craft knowledge.

Methodological considerations are also important here. The current study focused on questions about teachers' craft knowledge that were similar to but distinct from those addressed in the original study. The specific focus of the current study on teachers' thinking about what led to effective learning outcomes clearly required teachers to concentrate on a particular aspect of their craft knowledge that was only one part of their more global thinking about their teaching that was the focus of the earlier work. Some of the apparent differences in our findings, therefore, should be seen in terms of being different answers to different questions, and as such not inconsistent.

In the next two chapters we will further extend this exploration of teachers' craft knowledge, and show some of the ways in which it interacts with pupils' craft knowledge.

# 5 / Pupils' craft knowledge compared with that of teachers

Much of what has just been said about the nature of teachers' professional craft knowledge also applies to pupils' craft knowledge. As this chapter will show, students, like their teachers, have understandings about how to engage in the learning process. One element of teachers' craft knowledge would in fact appear to be a recognition of this, as we shall see, and it is clearly something that teachers in this study sometimes relied on.

Pupils' craft knowledge, like teachers', was concerned with a wide range of issues in which effective teaching and learning were nested. Like teachers, pupils were concerned with the teaching and learning context and had different strategies for getting through the succession of lessons that make up the school day. Just as teachers saw the 'management' of pupils as an important task, so students 'manage' one another and, to some extent, their teachers too. Pupils in the present study showed an adeptness in catering for the individual differences between their teachers, by adjusting their behaviour and conduct in response to their perceptions of different teacher characteristics. Knowing what their teacher 'liked', in terms of forms of behaviour, and patterns of classroom engagement were vital aspects of pupil craft knowledge. Our concern, however, is with the craft knowledge embodied in pupils' attempts to learn effectively the subjects they were being taught.

As will be shown, chief constructs in students' craft knowledge were often complementary with teachers' constructs when associated with effective learning outcomes. For students, their opportunities for engaging in effective learning depended upon the existence of certain conditions relating to cognitive, social and affective factors. When teachers created the appropriate conditions students were able to apply their preferred learning strategies and means of engagement; they would, however, restrict their engagement where conditions were not felt to be congenial. This was illustrated by a student who claimed that the way in which she had engaged in a creative writing project had been influenced by her perception of the teacher involved. Comparing her current teacher with a previous teacher, she explained that had the former, unsympathetic and bullying, teacher asked her to carry out the same task she would have approached it with less personal openness for fear of the critical response she might receive. The current teacher, however, projected a warm persona so that the student felt able to articulate personal thoughts and feelings without fear. This indicates the extent to which this student saw the social and affective climate as a vital ingredient in the learning process. Without the appropriate social and affective conditions she would not have engaged in the process as fully as she knew herself to be capable.

Clearly pupils do not, automatically, have control over the conditions in which they are expected to learn. Neither do teachers. In so far as teachers and pupils form highly significant aspects of each others' working environment, it is clearly the case – and this will be demonstrated below – that the working context is to a significant degree the product of negotiation between teachers and pupils. The negotiation can be seen in terms of an interaction between teachers' and pupils' versions of craft knowledge. Pupils' craft knowledge, it will be shown, revolves around issues of personal engagement and the perceived need to integrate school knowledge with their existing knowledge and ways of understanding. As the previous example indicates, a powerful negotiating tool for pupils is their willingness to engage, and it might be hypothesized that they reward teachers who create opportunities for congenial classroom interaction with their engagement. We see this illustrated in our discussion of 'reactive teaching' in Chapter 6.

### Similarities and differences in teachers' and students' concerns with classroom outcomes

In this section we examine in detail the kinds of outcomes that teachers and students described as seeking in lessons.

Like teachers, students often showed an awareness of long- and short-term outcomes. Pupils, however, tended to be mostly concerned with short-term outcomes. When describing subject specific outcomes, pupils in general focused on short-term outcomes that were specific to and contained within a particular lesson. They rarely talked about their learning in relation to long-term issues, such as examinations or the aims of the National Curriculum, as their teachers did. Thus, it was common for pupils to be able to give an account of the way in which a particular task or illustration in a lesson related to a specific learning point, such as when a history teacher employed a story about a car accident to illustrate the nature of short- and long-term consequences of historical events. On a few occasions pupils did refer to longer-term outcomes by indicating that learning outcomes would serve a valuable purpose in the future, or in relation to some context outside the school situation. Examples of this were when pupils related their learning to life skills or job-related skills. One pupil described the value of a lesson in which he had been required to write a letter as providing him with knowledge he would draw on the next time he wrote a letter out of school.

Commonality in relation to teachers' and pupils' perceptions of classroom outcomes varied in a number of ways. It is possible to classify the types of outcomes talked about by teachers and pupils into two broad categories. The first category is 'learning outcomes' and the second category is a general category covering social and personal outcomes, including perceived states of affairs that teachers and students considered to have important consequences for learning. By and large there was a greater tendency among pupils than teachers to refer to specific learning outcomes from lessons, as primary concerns.

*Similarities and differences in relation to learning outcomes*

When speaking about learning outcomes teachers often talked in terms of skills and understanding exhibited by pupils:

> Technically, em, I think they'd established different ways of drafting: making notes, writing from best, and they began to understand what drafting is . . . we talked about reliability of evidence . . . some of them are getting on quite well with that idea; they are understanding those concepts quite well already.

When students talked about learning outcomes they too sometimes spoke about skills and understanding:

> I didn't really know about how they [historians] worked [in] history, and how we find out about history. [I now understand that] somebody tells somebody . . . somebody tells somebody else what happened. The story's going to change. But they go back and find evidence if it's happened like the police do.

The recurrence of technical terms introduced in lessons in both teacher and student accounts indicated that there were important links between teacher input and the terms in which teachers framed learning outcomes. This phenomenon recurred throughout the interview transcripts. This would appear to be evidence suggesting that pupils' talk about their learning was, at these times, derivative of the language used by teachers. This can, in turn, be related to teachers' often deliberate highlighting and reinforcement of specific items of vocabulary, in both English and history.

In another example we saw how teacher and student perceptions of learning outcomes diverged in subtle ways. In this lesson the teacher had given the students the task of summarizing the causes of Julius Caesar's assassination, as they were represented in a textbook, and then listing them in order of importance. The teacher described the outcome of the lesson in terms of student performance and inferred learning outcomes from this:

> I was quite pleased with the way they thought about it, because look-ing around at the way they'd rearranged the list on their tables . . . most of them had actually put what I would consider to be the more im-portant ones at the top . . . they seemed to sort that out in quite a good way . . . I mean that's just starting them off on the idea that there are lots of reasons for something happening, and that some reasons are more important than others.

When a student was interviewed about this lesson she claimed to have learned: 'Different ways how he was murdered.' She also went on to de-scribe how certain skills she had developed in the course of this lesson might be of more general benefit in her future historical studies, such as the study of the Second World War: 'We know how Hitler was killed, but if we didn't, we could do the same thing that we did with Julius Caesar, if he had been murdered . . . [There are] probably lots of reasons [why Hitler killed himself] . . . There might just have been one reason. We don't know.' We find the student's account of outcomes somewhat inconclusive as a means of assessing the extent to which she achieved the outcomes described by her teacher. On the one hand, her focus was on the literal content of the lesson: she absorbed knowledge about the causes of Cae-sar's death. This, however, was an outcome that the teacher did not mention. On the other hand, the student shared with her teacher a per-ception of the transferability of the skills she has practised in this lesson. But the 'basic idea', cited by the teacher, that 'there are lots of reasons for something happening', is not as firmly held by the student as the teacher appeared to expect. The student did not generalize from her study of Caesar's death that there are many reasons for events. Rather, she be-lieved she had learned a technique for ordering multiple causes in order of importance; it was only 'probable' that other historical events will have multiple causes.

The subtle disparity between the student and teacher accounts of learning outcomes was frequently reflected in other cases across both subjects. As this example illustrates, students most often talked about their learning in terms of the acquisition of factual information, or in terms of their mastery of instrumental skills. Where divergence took place this often related to issues of abstraction and concreteness. Where the teacher gave an account that indicated a conceptual learning outcome (such as the formal nature of the drafting process), pupils whose accounts were different tended to focus on what they saw as concrete skills that they had learned and would be able to reproduce at a later date. Similarly, where teachers saw subtle correspondences between different concepts that could be used to make generalizations, pupils sometimes described more literal correspondences. This is illustrated above in the account of the pupil who compares the death of Caesar with that of Hitler.

The commonality in teachers' and students' ways of speaking about their learning experiences indicates a convergence in their thinking about subjects which is often attributed by students to teacher input in lessons, either direct input, through oral and/or visual presentation, or indirect input, through, for example, pupil use of resources that the teacher has directed pupils to. The evidence of divergent perceptions of learning outcomes, however, points to the presence of a more active approach to learning among students, who, on these occasions, would appear to be engaging in their own sense-making activities, independently, to a large extent, of teacher action and direction. This is illustrated in divergent perceptions of an English lesson where students were instructed to produce their own 'passports' as part of an autobiography. The teacher described the learning outcomes in terms of students' mastery of the techniques involved in redrafting, while a student described the major learning experience of the lesson in terms of learning how to fill in a passport application form 'when we get older [and] we get our own passport.' He too referred later to having employed drafting as an incidental, instrumental process. We might hypothesize that in instances such as this, students are motivated to attend to aspects of the lesson which they perceive as coinciding with their own agenda of concerns and interests.

*Similarities and differences in relation to other classroom outcomes: normal desirable states and 'working well'*

The second category of outcomes relates in particular to classroom states and events which were perceived by teachers and pupils to be valuable, either as being conducive of learning or other desirable longer-term outcomes, or as valuable for other reasons. Teachers and pupils talked of such events and states not simply as processes, but as valuable achievements or outcomes themselves. These outcomes would appear to correspond closely with Brown and McIntyre's (1993) concept of normal desirable states. Under this heading was a range of behaviours which were judged by teachers and pupils to relate to learning, pupils' social behaviour, the quality of social interaction and the general social climate in the classroom. Other outcomes related to pupils' affective states, both inferred from pupil behaviour and as experienced by pupils, and the products of classroom processes, such as pupils' verbal performance and other 'work' products. Teachers, in particular, also employed a concept of 'progress', in relation to the quality of work and the rate at which it was done in the classroom.

An important criterion applied by teachers and students when talking about the success of a particular lesson was the notion of 'working well'. Whether or not students were 'working well' was often determined on the basis of observed or self-reported behaviour. 'Working well' involved engaging in on-task behaviour in an appropriate way. A history teacher provided an example of how such on-task behaviour was sometimes associated with student learning and understanding. She was describing the students' performance in a question and answer session she conducted after her reading aloud the story of Thomas Becket's murder:

> I was quite pleased with that; they did pick out some quite good things from that . . . when we did those newspapers for English, we talked about the language bias and the word 'murder' had come out before as a very loaded word. So [in the lesson on Becket] they'd remembered that, which was good.

Sometimes, however, 'working well' could be quite independent of desired learning outcomes, as a second history teacher demonstrated:

> The story of Romulus and Remus – I want to do it how I did it before, which was to divide the class up into groups of four . . . and then in their groups they carve up the story into sections. And what we ended up with was a piece of sugar paper with four A4 sheets on, with a picture and caption underneath in the right order, and told the story of Romulus and Remus. And that worked very well. I was very pleased with how they did that last year, and so I'm going to try that again with some sort of extra explanation about paying attention to the story, because there were some rather strange pictures that came out of it where they obviously hadn't listened very well.

Here, although what we might term the cognitive outcomes of the task were considered by the teacher to be unsatisfactory, the teacher still claimed that the task had 'worked very well'. In this case it was the teacher's belief that the pupils were engaging with the task in an appropriate way that was the main source of satisfaction. Apparently the affective outcomes of students having engaged cooperatively and with enjoyment were seen as providing sufficient justification for the task to be considered to have 'gone well', in spite of the fact that the cognitive objectives (relating to understanding of historical content) had in some cases not been met.

The emphasis on affective outcomes continues when we observe that discussion, group and pair work sessions were often judged in similar ways by teachers of both subjects, with criteria such as student 'liveliness', willingness to participate and responsiveness being employed by teachers.

Students and teachers shared a concern for the importance of discipline and listening skills in group discussion, as well as a recognition of the need for a balance between the distribution of time between teacher and student talk. Students complained when teachers tended to 'go on for too long', while teachers often claimed to ration their own talking time deliberately.

Another aspect of teachers' concern with the affective dimensions was shown by some teachers placing enormous stress on the way in which the teaching process contributed to the social climate of the classroom, as well as their students' perceptions of the subject being taught. The issue of teacher talk was seen as central to this, and could even be seen to influence the lesson content that teachers sometimes selected. A history teacher illustrated this point, when she talked about what she experienced as a tension in the emphasis placed by the National Curriculum history on historical skills as opposed to content. While she recognized the need to make students aware of the skills they were using, she was concerned that students' enthusiasm for the subject might be undermined by an over-emphasis on what she saw as the dry and over abstract nature of skill analysis: 'If I start going on [to pupils] about, "well, of course, you realize what we've been doing is a historical skill." And then launch into this long [lecture], they all switch off. I don't want them to do that, because I don't want them to think that history's got to be laboured.' As a consequence of this way of thinking this teacher decided to leave dormant the issue of which skills pupils had been practising in the work on the death of Caesar, preferring to revisit this in year 8 or 9.

Students often shared with teachers a common view of what it meant to 'work well', showing a concern for affective outcomes by citing the importance they attached to the ways in which students 'got on with one another' in groups, and technical outcomes when they referred to the extent to which group and pair discussions focused on the set task. Students often described criteria for the quality of group experience, good groups being ones where pupils cooperate with one another, listen to one another, maintain a focus on the task and divide responsibilities fairly. An important quality sought in fellow group members was the willingness to accept unattractive roles and responsibilities, in order to promote group cohesion and aid group progress. Teachers did not tend to talk about group membership qualities in such detail, tending to employ more global perspectives, and focusing on the outward indications of pupil cooperation and involvement.

The importance of students' affective states was repeatedly stressed. Both teachers and students often referred to student enjoyment or the experience of 'fun' as an important outcome which could lead to effective learning. A history teacher gave an example of this when she described the way she had used an extract from the script of *Monty Python's Life of Brian* to introduce the study of the Roman Empire: 'I do try quite hard to get them to enjoy their work, and I think sometimes if they have a bit of fun along the way, then they enjoy it and hopefully it sticks a bit more . . . hopefully they'll also realize that there is something serious about it as well.' It is interesting to note the relative weighting here between the teacher's recognition of the 'fun' aspect of the chosen resource material and her tentativeness with regard to its efficacy as a learning aid. As we saw above, many teachers placed a high value on student affect, and one English teacher declared the importance of pupil 'enjoyment' to be such that she ranked it among her major teaching objectives. All the teachers in the study expressed similar sentiments at different times, indicating, to differing degrees, that they saw part of their role as being ambassadors for their subjects, with a responsibility to present it in a positive and attractive light to their students.

## Classroom practices leading to learning

Above we have considered the ways in which teachers and pupils describe learning and other outcomes of classroom activity that they value. We now turn to a consideration of the teaching and learning strategies which they report as leading to these outcomes, and especially learning outcomes.

### Students' and teachers' preferred teaching and learning strategies

In this section we highlight some key features of students' craft knowledge, and show how these to some extent contrasted with teachers' views of effective teaching. Most notable in what follows is the importance that pupils attached to personal cognitive engagement with new knowledge. Some of the strategies that pupils used for this are demonstrated. This is shown in the context of teachers' much wider definition of effective teaching, which is seen to have encapsulated a wide range of considerations, of which pupil learning is only one.

Both teachers and pupils were deeply concerned with the means by which learning was facilitated in the classroom. There was strong agreement between teachers and pupils about the range of most effective teaching strategies and techniques. However, there were also important variations in the detailed perceptions of teachers and pupils which were likely to have consequences for teacher effectiveness.

Pupils and teachers both described situations in which the following methods were seen as valuable aids to learning and understanding:

- teacher making explicit the agenda for the lesson;
- teacher recapping on previous lesson, highlighting continuity between lessons;

- story telling (by teacher)*;
- reading aloud (by teacher/by pupils);
- teacher mediation and modification of pupil verbal input to class discussion/board work;
- oral explanation by teacher, often combined with discussion/question answer sessions* or use of blackboard*;
- blackboard notes and diagrams as *aide-mémoire*;
- use of pictures and other visual stimuli (for exploration/information)*;
- use of 'models' based on pupil work or generated by teacher;
- structure for written work generated and presented by teacher;
- group/pair work (for oral and practical purposes)*;
- drama/role play*;
- printed text/worksheets;
- use of stimuli which relates to pupil pop culture*.

(An additional strategy referred to by pupils only is pupil drawing.)

However, while many pupils favoured certain of these methods (the items followed by an asterisk) as particularly powerful learning aids, the teachers tended not to see these as distinctive. Rather, the teachers tended to take a more contextualized view, seeing different methods as being appropriate for different learning tasks, and being appropriate for reasons relating to prevailing conditions (such as time, nature and availability of resources, perceptions of the class, classroom management considerations, their view of the nature of their subject).

The important point to be made here is that pupils had preferred ways of engaging with and acquiring new knowledge and understanding, and these preferences were perceived by them to relate to the success of the learning experience; for teachers, on the other hand, the choice of teaching method was governed by a range of sometimes conflicting considerations, which may or may not relate to pupils' preferred approaches to learning. This meant that teachers sometimes employed methods which were not, in their view, most appropriate to the material:

> I can't afford to give more than this week to Thomas Becket. And anyway that's too much, because we've only got two weeks [until the end of term] . . . We're supposed to be doing the origins of parliament and the legacy of the Middle Ages . . . How do I get all that done in such a small space of time? . . . I'll probably show them a video of the Peasants' Revolt, or something.

The more immediate classroom context was also a powerful influence on teachers' choice of approach. This was illustrated by an English teacher, who described her reasons for shifting from a task combining reading and a whole class discussion to written work on the same subject (a narrative version of *The Tempest*):

I think it's fascinating . . . their response when I said, 'Right . . . we'll leave it there and do some writing.' 'Oooh!' [imitation of pupils' groans] As if you'd asked them to do the worst thing in the world . . . But I'm aware – I suppose it's classroom management . . . You become aware that some children have gone past the stage of wanting to hear what other people's ideas are . . . Just a few who were – people like Jimmy, who were obviously restless from the word go . . . and the odd other few, who were getting a bit fidgety. I felt it was time to actually get them to focus on writing something down.

In this example, the teacher's reasons for changing the task were not entirely related to the pupils' waning interest, but also to other pupils' apparent overenthusiasm for the topic:

Quite a few of them were getting restless because they were excited about what they were doing . . . and were obviously enjoying it. They were just going to get more and more high. And it would be hard to pull them back down to write down their homework, let alone write anything else down.

Another important consideration is the teacher's perceptions of the nature of the lesson content: 'I think any topic that involves issues, I would try to teach in a way that they were actually thinking for themselves, and making decisions about what they thought about it. I mean, you can't really do that sort of thing with medieval farming, can you!' Similarly, another history teacher accounted for her increased use of groupwork and greater exercise of pupil autonomy in terms of the topic of study:

It's because of the nature of what they're doing . . . That's the easiest way to do it. I mean the soap opera work was . . . at the start . . . didactic in terms of, 'OK . . . what's a soap opera? What do you know about soap operas?' And it was only during that soap opera work that the tables changed [i.e. the arrangement of desks in the classrooms was changed to facilitate greater pupil interaction than was permitted under the previous arrangement].

We found that teachers employed each of the methods listed above at different times in accordance with their perceptions of appropriateness in relation to the prevailing conditions and their wider aims. It should be stressed that some teachers included in these conditions assumptions about pupils' learning processes, as an English teacher shows when she talks about the use of classroom talk with her year 7 group: 'through talk, you make more specific in your own mind, so you clarify in your own mind what it is you wish to say . . . And I think that's happened with the children.' Another English teacher described the way in which he sought to provide learning experiences which catered for a wide range of pupil aptitudes:

> I always like to address the three profile components through every unit of work I do. There's got to be an element of reading, there's got to be an element of speaking and listening, there's got to be an element of writing . . . If we're defining mixed ability in terms of those who find writing difficult, then on the other hand, those who are competent oral communicators, then there'll be something in every new approach for every different member of the group . . . So I hope that . . . a variety of approach is . . . going to allow every member of the class to be involved with it in some way.

This teacher's pragmatic solution acknowledged the variety that is likely to exist in pupils' preferred approaches to learning, while taking as its starting point the contextual matter of the linguistic skills that are prescribed by the National Curriculum.

### Drama, role play and stories

Pupils' judgements of the effectiveness of teaching methods related almost exclusively to their personal experiences of learning. There were strong themes running through these pupil accounts which indicated that these pupils had good reasons for favouring certain teaching methods over others. Pupils recalled more readily lesson activities that they associate with a relatively high level of arousal. Pupils' accounts of their own most effective learning were associated with these same events. Invariably pupils describe a high degree of constructive participation in the events recalled. Accounts of such participation often revealed important links between the activities engaged in and pupils' knowledge and understanding of lesson content. In these circumstances, therefore, the learning that had taken place was linked to events in which the pupils had participated in some way, such as in a physical or imaginative sense. This was demonstrated vividly in the often cited dramatic reconstruction of the assassination of Julius Caesar, staged by a history teacher. Here we saw how a pupil's knowledge and understanding of this subject was linked to his recall of classroom events in which he had participated:

> We done about the killing of Julius Caesar, the assassination of Julius Caesar, and we done it in a sort of like play . . . in the classroom. We put all the tables back and we done all the speaking and that. Yeah, and I was one of the crowd . . . it was good, because everyone had brought sheets in and dressed up as Romans . . . I knew [i.e. learned] from that that they didn't want a king, because [they wanted] to stop Rome from going under again . . . Before they'd had a king and queen,

[and] they got a bit big for their boots, and they killed them, or something, and I didn't know that. And I knew that he [Caesar] was really brutally killed, because all the senate gathered round him and they each drew their daggers and stabbed him, and it said on something that he was stabbed 28 times.

The close association between the new knowledge and the setting, and the actual people with whom the pupil interacted during the lesson, is clearly demonstrated:

There was Terry, I think was Brutus, and he done a defence, why he killed Julius Caesar. And everybody liked him. And then John Anthony [*sic*], I think it was, came on and he sort of like slowly went against Brutus . . . and all the crowd ended up against him. And they went off saying that they'd burn his house and that. It was good! . . . I [am] sort of like remembering Simon standing up on the chair, speaking out, and I remember two people dragging on Julius Caesar, and I can remember Tracy, that was John Anthony – I can remember her showing the dagger wounds, because we had this special sheet that has dagger wounds in it. And another thing I learned from it was Julius Caesar's final words: 'Et tu Brute.' Which means, 'and you Brutus' . . . because he thought Brutus was his best friend. And Brutus ended up killing him; so he didn't like that very much!

This boy firmly believed that although some of his knowledge of this topic had been gathered from reading, that reading alone would have been ineffective. It was the drama which was the focal point of his appreciation of this topic; the reading was only valuable in a supplementary sense. 'Well, you take more notice when you [are] doing it in a play, than you do when you're sat there reading it. So you really listen hard, and it helps a lot.' An important feature of this account is the way in which the pupil's description of apparently irrelevant incidental details formed part of his recall. It is suggested that such incidental features provided important cues by which he was able to link the subject knowledge he described to his personal experience of taking part in a real event. This process can be seen as being central to this pupil's craft knowledge as a learner.

The pupil's account of the role play of the death of Caesar was typical of pupil responses to this lesson, which was repeatedly referred to by many pupils long after it had taken place. In fact there had been a ten-week gap between the lesson and the account of it reported here. Clearly, the extreme nature of the events portrayed in this example might be assumed to be an important cause here. However, we found similar effects with dramatizations of less extreme material, such as: a role play in which the division of Roman society into plebeians and patricians was enacted; the use of role play by an English teacher to demonstrate the appropriateness of register in face-to-face communication; the use of role play by another English teacher to portray the story lines of a series of narrative poems; and a role play in which pupils were required to discuss the pros and cons of taking part in the Peasants' Revolt. This would indicate that it was the method rather than the content that was the critical focus of pupils' claims of effectiveness.

This view of the power of role play was echoed in relation to other teaching methods and classroom experiences described by pupils as being successful. This is particularly true of their descriptions of the use of story telling and visual stimuli as teaching aids. In both cases these were seen to have a powerful effect on pupils' learning and understanding, and this effect seems to be related to the powerful imaginative impact of these stimuli.

There were two major categories of stories told by teachers that pupils found effective: stories which were intrinsically interesting by virtue of their content, and stories which appeared to reveal something of the personal lives of their teachers. In both cases pupils claim to be motivated to pay close attention by their desire for more information and the entertainment value of the experience. With regard to teachers' personal stories, this applied equally well to teachers' brief personal anecdotes, which were often used to illustrate a point. When recalling information during interviews pupils often did so most effectively when they followed the narrative patterns of the story as presented by the teacher. This suggests that the sequencing and other structural features of stories provide important cues for recall. Once again, this can be illustrated through the use of highly evocative material, such as the story of the murder of Becket, and by less dramatic means, such as a personal story told by a history teacher to illustrate the concepts of short-term and long-term consequences. This latter story was recalled by several pupils who when defining the nature of short- and long-term consequences did so by reconstructing events in the teacher's story.

The use of visual stimuli seems to have worked in a similar way to that of story and drama, in that it often seemed to provide pupils with a framework by which they were able imaginatively to reinstate information. The unit on the Black Death provided an interesting illustration of this point, showing how a pupil's close examination of a pictorial source stimulated his thinking about the subject, and how the combination of text and picture helped him to extend his knowledge (the picture was from a contemporaneous source and depicts Death as a skeleton riding a horse):

Well, the first thing I looked at was the skeleton, and I thought, 'Ugh! he doesn't look very nice . . . Then I looked all around the edges, and there was some rich people dying, and there was some holy people dying, reverends and stuff. And then on the other side, there was sort of like dark, in a dark colour; there was poor people dying. And he was riding on a horse, and the horse was trying to trample on the people as well, because the horse was jumping about all over. I noticed that all the streets were dirty, and some people, I think it was the Germans, thought it was a message from God, saying they hadn't behaved themselves properly . . . After people had read their sources [pupils read sections of the textbook aloud to the class] I started to look more closely [at the picture, for] fountains with dirty water and that.

Visual representation was not simply important in relation to the nature of stimuli material, it was itself a major element in the cognitive processes which some pupils reported employing during learning. A pupil provided a vivid example of this when he described the way in which he responded to the teacher's reading of the story of Becket's murder:

[While Ms Wills was reading the story I was] just like making pictures in my head of it, of what was happening. I was sort of thinking about Feddlestone [local village] church. I don't know why! . . . Picturing the church helps me know the scene and what's happening better . . . I remember four knights meeting and a man, he was a man and not a knight . . . he come down from some stairs, or come from a door, stood by a post. And they tried to drag him away, but they couldn't get him away from the post.

Another boy described a similar technique:

Well, [when] she's reading it out I was thinking about what it would have been like, and . . . when something interesting comes up I put that in my kind of play . . . [When the teacher told a story about a car crash] I did the same again, put myself in a car crash, went to court. And then we did it again with the Black Death, I did the same.

Both these pupils were describing their own ways of making sense of learning material. In both cases they imaginatively transform the teacher's input into their own terms of reference. This represents craft knowledge of how to engage with the learning task, based on experience and understanding of their own learning processes.

The theme of transformation was a powerful one in pupil accounts, to the extent that it could be said that a common thread throughout their accounts of the learning process was their reliance on transformation strategies. When pupils spoke of this they usually referred to circumstances where they forged connections between their past or present experience and teacher input. In the accounts of drama/role play activities, pictorial representation and story telling we found pupils engaging in what might be termed a process of concretization, whereby ideas which teachers presented were made distinct and given a meaning that was dependent on the context of their delivery; sometimes this context was chiefly provided by the teacher, at other times by the pupils. In either case, however, the pupils engaged actively in the process, by constructing the context (as with visualization techniques) or by bringing their experience and interest into focus (as in story telling, the use of visual aids and role play). The chief activity that pupils seemed to be engaging in is perhaps best termed one of appropriation. The activity of appropriation will now be further exemplified in relation to the remaining teaching methods that pupils identified as being distinctive in their effectiveness.

### Discussion, question–answer and pupil collaboration

While drama/role play, story telling and visual stimuli were considered by pupils to be important for their imaginative, visual and activity content, class discussion, teacher-led question and answer situations and group/pair work are taken together because of the importance that pupils placed on their own verbal participation in these classroom practices. Once again, however, interviewees emphasized the ways in which these contributed to pupil appropriation and construction of knowledge. From the pupil standpoint, the most valuable shared aspects of these approaches were the opportunities they created for pupils to generate and be exposed to new representations of knowledge and ideas, as well as providing possible confirmation or denial of their own ideas.

According to pupils, the most successful class discussions were often those which provided opportunities for autonomous thought and personal expression while being carefully directed by the teacher. In this example, the teacher (Ms Hall) punctuated the reading of a text with the whole class with a series of mini-discussions in which pupils shared speculations as to how the plot might develop:

> I like it how we're reading it, step by step, rather than just reading it all . . . So you can, like, really get into the story and guess what could happen next. It's more fun, rather than just reading page by page. There's more adventure in it, like the books we were reading in the library.

Emily was referring here to a series of interactive books in which the reader is required to make choices which determine the particular way in which the narrative develops. She found a sense of 'adventure' in this approach to the story. The 'adventure' lay in the mental challenge of unravelling the mystery of the story and in the possibility of confirmation or denial of their hypotheses as the story unfolds. The teacher's technique heightened the imaginative impact of the story, which in turn motivated the pupil to engage closely with the text. The theme of pupil involvement is strong here. The fact that pupils were required to articulate their ideas in the discussion phase, also acted as a stimulus for developing and fixing their ideas: 'Well, when she was reading, I thought of an idea, and then, when we were asked to do it [i.e. to give their ideas], it sort of really pinged up!'

The most important aspect of this situation, however, was the discussion itself, which acted as a stimulus to pupil thinking:

> [Whenever we stopped reading] I was thinking, like what was going to happen next. Because we started, like, where say something strange happened, and new people came into the story, and discussed what they'd be. And people [other pupils, came] with ideas of what's going to happen next . . . [Other pupils] were asking questions. Like they'll remind us about something that happened at the beginning [of the story], and they'll go, 'Oh yeah, that happened.' And when they gave the ideas it gave you one as well; to help you to what you were thinking.
>
> (Sean)

This genuine sharing of ideas helps pupils to deepen their knowledge and understanding of the text, by encouraging them to reflect on and develop their own ideas:

*Emily:* It's good, I prefer lessons like that instead of just, like, doing work from a book, because I like discussions and things.

*Sean:* Yeah. Because you can see other people's point of view about the story and share your own [view] . . .

*Emily:* [I enjoyed having] other people agree with you, and [when] they thought it was a good idea [if they didn't agree with you] they would explain why they didn't think it was a good idea, and all that, and I wouldn't have thought of that, so I would agree with them.

Emily and Sean exemplified the way in which their own thinking had developed through discussion, both with reference to the lesson and through a demonstration in the course of the interview. They were referring to a section of the lesson in which they had discussed why Prospero should want to send Ariel to bring Ferdinand to him:

*Emily:* One [pupil] was saying . . . 'So that they could like kidnap him' . . . Somebody else had an idea, like he [Ferdinand] could marry my [Prospero's] daughter if you [Ferdinand] tell me about your dad: where he is and everything. So he could find out and then he could go and get her. So I've got your son trapped, so let me have my throne back.

*Sean:* Yeah, but he [Ferdinand] didn't know that Prospero was there. He thought that Prospero was dead, ages ago. Because it said like [in the text], 12 years later, when Caliban – six years later – so it was

a long time after. He'd forgotten about his brother, and didn't
know what he looked like so –
*Emily:* And Prospero loved his daughter, so I don't think he would have
done that to her: like, make her fall in love with Ferdinand.

Emily's starting point in this extract was her recollection of a contribution
made to the lesson by an unnamed pupil. This stimulated Sean to cite
textual detail which might support the hypothesis. Emily, however, responded to Sean by presenting an opposing view based on an imaginative
projection from the text. This extract strongly supports the claim of the
effectiveness of discussion as a means of encouraging pupils to formulate
and articulate ideas on the basis of a close reading of text. The pupils'
automatic slipping into discussion mode during the interview itself indicated the power of this technique: these pupils were clearly highly stimulated by the activity and showed an exuberance in their performance of
this skill.

Another interesting feature of this extract was the way in which Emily,
in the opening lines, quickly switched from the use of the third person to
the first person when describing Prospero's possible motives, indicating
the extent of her imaginative involvement with the text, and hinting at the
type of cognitive process that she may employ in approaching these
questions. This offers support to assertions that have already been made
about the way in which some pupils appeared to 'concretize' ideas. The
elements of fun and active engagement that these pupils exhibited are not
to be underestimated as factors contributing to the success of this strategy.

Pupils and teachers indicated that group and pair work operated in very
similar ways to discussion, though there are important distinctions to be
made. While the patterns of interaction and the progress of work tended
to be structured by the teacher in whole-class discussions, in groupwork
pupils took responsibility for these areas, and the extent to which pupils
were successful in dealing with these formed an important part of both
teachers' and pupils' perceptions of the success of groupwork. As a pupil
suggested in his description of an English lesson in which his group had
been required to devise and write a play script, '[Our group worked] quite
well, actually. Because we got a lot done, and we figured what we were
doing in the story straight away. There was no arguing about the title.'

Pupils were virtually unanimous in describing the major value of groupwork as being, like class discussion, that it widened the pool of available
ideas, and through this, enabled pupils to advance their thinking in ways
which they could not achieve alone. This use of the multiple perspectives
provided by group members also manifested itself in other ways, such as
in the mediation of teacher input to group processes. There were several
examples provided by pupils, in which different pupils contributed to the
group at different times an input based upon instruction given by the

teacher earlier in the lesson. In this way the group acts as a kind of super-memory on which it draws as the need arises, with each pupil being custodian of a slightly different set of recollections of teacher or other input. Furthermore, the teacher input was often rendered more access-ible to many pupils by being rephrased by pupils into 'pupil speak' (see below).

Pair work was experienced as having similar benefits to groupwork, with the exception that it was more often cited as offering pupils a personal rehearsal function, in that they were often required to use pair work for purposes of articulating ideas and hypotheses prior to some form of written or oral performance. Both pair and groupwork also provided pupils with opportunities for informal peer tutoring, which they found extremely valuable, particularly when they experienced learning difficulties.

A powerful feature uniting all these preferred strategies was the op-portunities they all provided for pupils to represent information in ways that they found personally meaningful. This is true of the more personal modes, such as imaginative enactment and visualization, and of the more social/verbal strategies, such as discussion and groupwork. A commonly repeated claim by pupils, for example, was that where pupils have difficulty understanding points presented by teachers, they often benefit from hearing the same point rephrased by a fellow pupil in terms that are more familiar to them. This worked in the opposite way sometimes, with teachers 'refining' pupils' verbal contributions and making their ideas more acces-sible to the rest of the group. Similarly, teachers' questions sometimes enabled pupils to articulate understandings of which they were not conscious.

The final strategy to be dealt with in this section is that of 'drawing'. This was not a highly valued activity by the teachers in this study, but it was considered to be a valuable learning medium by some pupils, particularly in history. There were repeated references to detailed knowledge of various historical situations that pupils attributed to their experience of having drawn them. Examples of this included knowledge about Roman villas, Roman weaponry and battle tactics. It is suggested that 'drawing' combines many of the qualities which have been attributed to other favoured strategies, in that it involves the representation of information in the pupil's own (graphic) terms, it involves visual representation and it requires the active participation of pupils. The importance of this active aspect of pupils' response to learning was underlined by a pupil when he said: '[English and history] they're better than most subjects where you're not doing anything. [They're] like games and design and technology.' This view, however, did not accord with that expressed by the teachers. English and history teachers saw themselves as drawing on strategies which involved pupils in practical ways when appropriate to the subject matter under consideration. Their subjects were perceived to be defined by their content, not the method.

And as a method, drawing was felt to be of limited value in the eyes of these teachers. We might speculate that this omission has something to do with the non-verbal quality of drawing, which distinguishes it from the other agreed strategies.

# 6 / Interactions between teacher and pupil craft knowledge

We have now looked at teachers' and pupils' sometimes differing ways of construing effective teaching and learning, and also delineated some of the elements of the craft knowledge that they bring to bear on the classroom learning. This chapter now takes a closer look at some of the ways in which teachers' and pupils' classroom thinking interacted to produce what teachers and pupils thought of as effective learning. As the chapter develops we also relate our theorizing to estabished theories of the socio-cultural nature of teaching and learning, drawing on the work of Bruner and Vygotsky.

The central question of this chapter is: how did teachers and pupils *work together* in ways that they considered effective for learning? We have seen that they were in agreement about a range of teaching methods which they saw as facilitating effective learning. We also saw, however, that teachers were influenced by a much wider range of concerns than pupils, and that they valued and used a wider range of teaching methods, from which they chose according to circumstances. We have also seen, in Chapter 4, that factors pertaining to their pupils, including pupils' perceived moods, attitudes and interests, were the most prominent kinds of circumstantial factors, among many others, to which teachers attended. It was also shown that goals concerned with pupil affect were prominent among those sought by teachers.

It is clear that the classroom actions taken by teachers were experienced by pupils as facilitating or constraining to varying degrees their opportunities for engaging in what they considered effective learning activities. It is also clear that teachers tended to be keenly aware of this, but also alert to many other considerations, such as time constraints, externally imposed curriculum and assessment requirements, and the different perceived needs of pupils in their classes. What is as yet unclear, however, is the nature of teachers' practical thinking, according to which they allowed (or did not allow) pupils' interests, preferences, enthusiasms and ideas to shape their teaching. The question is: how did it shape their teaching? Were pupils able to influence teachers' activities in ways calculated to facilitate their own learning? If so, how and in what circumstances? How were teachers able to take advantage of pupils' agendas in fostering the kind of learning which they sought to promote?

These are the kinds of questions with which this chapter is concerned. We are here, then, dealing with questions of 'bi-directionality', which, as noted in Chapter 1, have tended to be neglected in classroom research. Our concern is focused, however, on those influences of teachers and pupils on each others' classroom activities which stem from their conscious efforts to influence and to use the opportunities that the other provides for them. How do they interact to achieve effective teaching and learning?

It was not at all self-evident, in looking at our evidence, what kinds of patterns it might be possible to discern or in what terms it might be possible and useful to describe the interaction of teachers' and pupils' thinking. Initially, therefore, we tried to categorize teachers' and pupils' accounts of lessons in very simple terms, emphasizing *what* aspects of pupils' thinking or perceived states were reported as having influenced teachers' actions and *how* such pupil influence on teachers' actions had or had not contributed to the effectiveness of teaching and learning. In the following two sections we will seek to illustrate some of the ways in which pupils influenced teachers.

## Pupils' influences on teachers' actions

Teachers' actions in lessons were sometimes actively influenced by pupils. And effective teaching and learning, as identified by pupils and teachers, was often associated with claims that pupils influenced the lessons so that they were in tune with one of the following concerns:

- pupils' interests;
- pupils' knowledge and understanding;
- pupils' motivation;
- pupils' preferred ways of working;
- pupils' preferred styles of learning;
- pupils' expectations.

Sometimes teachers planned their lessons to allow pupils to influence the shape of the lesson; at other times the teacher modified his or her pre-lesson plan in response to pupil influence. Particular ways in which pupils influenced teachers' actions included:

- choice of learning activities;
- choice of teaching strategy;
- choice of resources;
- pacing of lessons.

Pupils expressed their interests, concerns and preferences in different ways, depending on the circumstances of the lesson. Sometimes pupils introduced artefacts into lessons, in the form of documents or objects brought from home. Sometimes this was in response to a request from the teacher, at other times it was a spontaneous pupil gesture. An example of the former was when an English teacher asked pupils to bring a small object of their own choice into the lesson that could be used as a prop in a story telling session. An example of the latter was when a pupil brought a Cornish language dictionary to a lesson, during a unit dealing with dialect and Standard English. In the case of the lesson on story telling the teacher gauged the level of pupil interest in the topic: (a) on the basis of the number of pupils who brought objects to the lesson; and (b) on the basis of the degree to which pupils seemed to express spontaneous interest in the objects they had brought. Because pupil interest and enthusiasm was unexpectedly high, she modified her original lesson plan by devoting much more time to class discussion of the objects and oral story telling than she had planned. As a consequence of apparent pupil interest, therefore, what had been planned as a writing activity became an oral activity. The incident relating to the Cornish language dictionary is dealt with in detail later in this chapter. The key point illustrated by this incident, however, is that the teacher devised an introduction to the lesson based on the use of the dictionary.

Pupils' existing knowledge and understanding was also used as a basis for teacher decision-making about lesson content on some occasions. This was particularly true in the early interactions between teachers and their new year 7 classes, where teachers often declared one of their intentions to be to ascertain the pupils' levels of skills and understandings. Having engaged in such an exercise in a unit on autobiography, for example, one English teacher devoted a number of lessons to issues of paragraphing and sentence structure.

One of the more proactive areas of pupil influence was in relation to ways of working. Although teachers often prescribed the ways in which pupils should work, they sometimes modified, and, in some cases, altered completely their plans for how pupils should work on a given subject in response to pupil requests. A relatively common scenario here was that teachers defined a task as essentially individual and non-collaborative, while pupils sought ways of making it collaborative. On other occasions what the teacher defined as a collaborative task was individualized at the request of pupils. Examples of the former occurred when teachers set written tasks, such as in a history lesson when the teacher asked pupils to answer written questions based on a passage. In these circumstances pupils often asked the teacher if they could work in pairs or small groups in order to complete the task. The latter situation of a collaborative task being converted into an individualized task for some pupils occurred less commonly. An example of this included a play writing task which the teacher had set up as a small group activity. One group was conspicuous in making extremely slow progress with the task. Eventually two members of this group approached the teacher and explained that their group could not reach consensus about a story line for their play; they asked to be allowed to work individually, and the teacher agreed to this.

Pupils' requests for specific activities were sometimes related to preferences for certain learning styles. As was noted in Chapter 5, pupils often showed a preference for learning activities that enabled them to engage in fairly concrete terms. This is reflected in requests that pupils sometimes made to be allowed (for example) to perform role plays, engage in discussion, draw pictures or otherwise develop an existing activity into one which involved a different style of cognitive engagement from that originally defined by the teacher. On the other hand, pupils sometimes asked if they could do a piece of writing based on a drama or other non-written activity. The preference for certain kinds of learning activity (for example, drama) was expressed by pupils to teachers verbally, and teachers were often very aware of pupils' expectations for such activities and catered for these accordingly.

## Pupils' influence on the perceived effectiveness of teaching and learning

Teachers' and pupils' claims for the relationship between such pupil influence and effectiveness, in terms of teaching and learning, suggest that pupil influence, at times, made an important contribution to learning in specific cases. This is particularly the case when we focus on the influence of pupils' interests, preferred ways of working and preferred styles of learning, in relation to teachers' choice of learning activities and choice of teaching strategy.

Where pupils' interests were part of the focus for learning activities pupils were able to recall lesson content with considerable vividness. In these circumstances pupils recalled the experience of the lesson in terms of their personal involvement. We noted a number of examples of the effect of this involvement on learning outcomes in Chapter 5. A particularly powerful effect was often attributed to the use of pupil collaboration strategies, whereby pupils engaged in dialogue with one another and

through this process helped one another to clarify teacher output or textual matter by transforming it into their own, more accessible, terms.

## Bi-directionality in teacher–student influence

One important issue here is that of 'bi-directionality' (Shavelson *et al.* 1986)
in teacher–pupil influence in the classroom. At its simplest, bi-directionality
is concerned with the ways in which teachers' strategies and behaviours
influence their pupils, and pupils' strategies and behaviours influence
their teachers. In proposing the idea that such recursive patterns of influence are important aspects of the classroom process, we are attempting
to move towards the development of a theoretical framework that will
incorporate and possibly extend existing research perspectives in the areas
of teachers' classroom thinking (e.g. Clark and Peterson 1986; Calderhead
1987) and pupils' classroom thinking (e.g. Schunk and Meece 1992). In
general, much existing research tends to focus on either teachers' or
pupils' influence on the learning situation (e.g. Levine and Wang 1983).
Research that has dealt with the interaction of these perspectives has tended
to focus on the effects of teachers' perceptions and strategies on pupil
outcomes (e.g. Brophy and Good 1986), or on the role of pupil cognition
in the mediation of teaching (Shulman 1986). The neglect of the issue of
bi-directionality in teacher–pupil influence is reflected in the dearth of
research that addresses this issue (Shavelson *et al.* 1986).

In this chapter we describe key patterns of teacher–pupil interaction
and influence in the classroom teaching and learning processes, with particular reference to the manifestation of this interaction in teachers'
classroom thinking. We also seek to illustrate the way in which our findings
can be seen to support a *transactional* theory of learning as proposed by
Vygotsky (1987) and Bruner (e.g. Bruner and Haste 1987).

## The transactional nature of teaching and learning

There is a strong sense in which both teachers and pupils in this study saw
effective teaching and learning as 'transactional' processes (Bruner 1987).
To a large extent their views of learning conformed to a model proposed
by Bruner and Haste (1987), which describes learning as a complex 'inter-
weaving' of 'language, interaction and cognition'. According to this model,
learning involves the sharing and testing of intersubjective meanings and
the negotiation of interpretations through interaction and the exercise
of empathy (taking the role of other). The teacher's role is to create
circumstances which enable the learner 'to integrate her capacities and
interpretations with those of significant others around her' (Bruner and

Haste 1987: 5). This is achieved (a) through the provision of *gramm*
*scripts*, and (b) through the process of *scaffolding*.

Grammars and scripts define appropriate ways of proceeding, behaviourally and linguistically, in a given situation. They are the patterns of expression and behaviour that are used by the pupil for 'making sense' of learning situations. The teacher provides them through direct instruction or by legitimizing the pupil's 'own behaviours and utterances' (Bruner and Haste 1987: 20).

Scaffolding is the process whereby the teacher provides model structures that enable the pupil to apply existing skills in new ways in the appropriation of new knowledge. The concept of 'scaffolding' would appear to be closely associated with Vygotsky's (1987) formulation of the *zone of proximal development* (ZPD), which crystallizes the underlying principle of Bruner and Haste's view of cognitive development as being highly dependent on socio-cultural influences. The ZPD describes the range of cognitive functions that can be achieved by the child when he or she is being guided by an adult or collaborating with more advanced peers, as opposed to those more limited functions that the child is capable of without such guidance or opportunities for collaboration. Scaffolding, then, is the extension to the child's capabilities that is afforded when the teacher instructs the pupil in procedures that enable him or her to employ existing skills in a new way in order to solve a problem. For example, scaffolding describes the process whereby a maths teacher helps a pupil to calculate the area of a triangle by responding to the pupil's own efforts and commentary on them, and by offering action suggestions that draw on the pupil's ideas. Thus if the pupil is trying to make use of her already developed understanding of how to calculate the area of rectangles, and of the use of rectangles as building-blocks, talk from the teacher in terms of half-rectangles may provide helpful scaffolding; but that will be so only if the pupil is already able to relate the idea of area to that of a half-rectangle. Otherwise, more basic scaffolding and indeed a shift to a different problem may be necessary. In English an example might be the extension of a pupil's compositional skills through the presentation of a 'beginning, middle and end' structure. The child is already able to write continuous, imaginative prose; the provision of this structure enables the child to incorporate structural considerations in the planning of compositions and thus to extend the range of literary devices already possessed.

The emphasis on the importance of socio-cultural factors that is inherent in a transactional theory of learning also leads us to consideration of a further area of concern that is common to the theories of learning that emerge from this study: that of *affect*. If we accept that learning is claimed to be dependent on certain types of interpersonal and social interaction, it follows that circumstances that make these forms of interaction desirable or at least congenial become a necessary prerequisite of effective learning. Furthermore, it can be argued that the appropriate forms of interaction that this view of learning considers necessary are dependent on the quality of the individual's self-image: his or her sense of self-worth and belief in his or her ability to take on and contribute to the resolution of problems. This requires an ego-supportive environment, in which the learner feels valued and respected by the significant others with whom he or she is expected to interact in the learning process.

An important mechanism within this transactional model of learning is *calibration* (Bruner 1987), which describes the careful development of intersubjectivity. Calibration occurs when teachers and pupils test their understandings against those held by the other, and adjust their utterances in order to make them accessible to each other. It is the process of transforming one's knowledge in a way that makes it accessible to others, and of actively appropriating others' knowledge in our own terms. This key mechanism draws attention to the goal-directedness of participants' thinking and behaviour.

The rest of this chapter is devoted to a more detailed explication of these processes as they relate to the first-hand experiences of effective teaching and learning as they are described by participants in our study. It will be shown that when the teachers and students in the present study talked about effective teaching and learning as they experienced it, they reflected, in their common-sense accounts, a complex knowledge of the ways in which social, cognitive and affective aspects of classroom interaction contributed to teaching and learning outcomes. This will be illustrated through reference to teachers' and students' accounts of what they consider to be the important purposes and outcomes of classroom teaching and learning, and their accounts of the means by which these are most effectively achieved. A major part of this chapter is, therefore, devoted to an account of teaching patterns that have been identified. These are reactive teaching and interactive teaching. It will be shown that these patterns are essentially 'transactional' in nature, through reference to the theoretical position presented above.

### Teacher strategies

When teachers talked about effective teaching that led directly to student learning they often talked in terms of the ways in which their pedagogical decisions were informed by perceptions they had (i.e. 'knowledge') of their students. Success often seemed to depend on the extent to which teachers effectively integrated their knowledge of students with other knowledge – such as knowledge of subject content, curriculum requirements and different possible ways of giving students access to this knowledge – into their overall teaching plans. The manner in which teachers managed this integration is best seen in terms of a continuum of teaching strategies that involved at one end *interactive* teaching, and at the other *reactive* teaching. When engaging in interactive teaching, the teacher integrated knowledge of students with preactive plans, in a way that placed the main emphasis on preset learning goals and the demands of the curriculum. When engaging in reactive teaching, teachers evolved plans more directly from their knowledge of students. Reactive teaching was characterized by the teacher's willingness to adjust learning objectives in order to accommodate student interests and intentions. Much of the time teachers seemed to engage in teaching that placed them somewhere towards the mid-point of the continuum, such as when teachers consciously and deliberately reacted to students' concerns and interests at the preactive stage in the formulation of lesson plans, or when teachers introduced minor modifications to lessons plans at the interactive stage in direct response to emergent student concerns or interests.

It should be stressed that the interactive–reactive continuum represented merely a segment of the wider continuum of teacher strategies. At the extreme end of the continuum beyond interactive teaching were *transmission strategies*, while at the extreme beyond reactive teaching were *strategies designed to facilitate self-directed learning*. The dynamic of this continuum was the degree to which teachers shared with students control over the learning situation, and the degree to which certain areas of decision-making were left open to negotiation.

*Interactive teaching*

The interactive end of the continuum can be illustrated with reference to the work of any of the teachers in this study. A particularly good example is provided by an English teacher who expressed a high degree of satisfaction with the learning outcomes he had observed from a unit concerned with 'knowledge about language' (KAL). In his summing up of the unit, he indicated a consciously strong commitment to what we term 'interactive teaching':

> [I was] pleased with the motivation of all the kids, and the way in which they brought, very enthusiastically, their own knowledge, or their own interest to that [i.e. the lesson content]. And the way in which they sparked ideas off each other, and started talking about issues to do with language that I hadn't necessarily introduced. And they seemed to have got a good understanding of the key terms that I tried to convey to them, in that sense. And now they talk quite confidently about 'jargon' and 'slang' and 'Standard English' and 'dialect'. And all I wanted to do, really, was to foster an awareness of those basic terms so when they go to new texts, they might think about that more.

It is quite clear that this teacher planned his teaching in such a way as to foster a transactional pattern of teaching and learning. An important mechanism for achieving this was the initiation and reinforcement of certain student scripts (Bruner and Haste 1987), which contained directions as to how students should contribute to lessons. One 'student contribution script' required pupils to bring items into lessons which had some bearing on the already planned lesson content:

> I always work like that. I always think that if children bring things to lessons which are going to help you along in a particular way, then you ought to use them. I think you ought to use them for two reasons. First of all, because it gives a positive message to the kids that a lesson is not just a teacher giving and children receiving [script reinforcement]. And that it's a two-way process, and that teachers can learn from children, and that it's a sharing and facilitating . . . Particularly in English, I think, because you're exploring things rather than having great bodies of knowledge [scaffolding]. So it's a positive thing, and I think it motivates them. And I like it from that point of view. But secondly, if you don't do that [i.e. utilize pupil material] I think you may well fall into the trap of teacher expectation, whereby you are too fixed in your own path, and you are determined to guide the class down a certain path. And if they say, 'Hey! This is interesting. Can't we stop and look at this for a little bit?' To say 'no' to that is unthinkable, because the teacher's being too rigid in their planning, and forcing the class down certain particular roads. Now I know that you have to have those planned out in your planning, and you have to take children in certain directions, because you've got objectives to meet, but if the things they're bringing in are stimulating and helpful, then I think it's a good idea to do that [i.e. utilize them].

The teacher clearly saw the use of reinforcement as essential to the establishment of the 'student contribution script' as an important part of the classroom process. He also described here a form of 'scaffolding' in that he appeared to be using this script to model a particular way of construing learning in English, as two-way and collaborative. This approach is distinctively *interactive* because, in this case, the teacher saw the proper use of pupil input as being only within the parameters set by his preactive lesson plans: 'if they ask questions like, "Can we look at this?", if I can see a way of fitting it into the [pre-planned] structure, well then the answer is usually "Yes, we can."'

Good examples of this type of interactive teaching were provided by this teacher during the KAL unit referred to above. The opening lesson of the unit was planned to centre on consideration of a number of poems written in various dialect forms. The teacher had already signalled in an earlier lesson that the lesson would be concerned with dialect by setting the class the homework task of making a list of some of the dialect terms that they and their families used. An unexpected consequence of this was that at the very beginning of the lesson a pupil presented to the teacher a Cornish language dictionary. As a result of this, the teacher structured his introduction to the lesson in such a way as to incorporate the newly introduced material. His procedure was to consult the dictionary, and then write three of the Cornish words on the blackboard ('mosow' meaning 'table', 'pluven' meaning 'pen', and 'paperyow' meaning 'paper') without their standard English translations. He then instructed the class to 'Get out your paperyow and pluven, and put them on your mosow.' His own account of the thinking behind these actions illustrates his intentions to legitimate certain student responses and so help them develop certain insights into the nature of language:

> That wasn't planned, because I'd only been presented with the material when I walked through the door, as a result of the . . . previous homework. [The pupil said] 'I got this [Cornish dictionary] from my mum.' And it was thrust right under my nose. I hadn't planned that, but I just thought: 'I'll have to start the lesson in that way.'

He adopted the particular strategy of using these Cornish words in order to facilitate students' appreciation of the 'fun' aspect of language study, and thereby introduced and endorsed the idea that 'students can enjoy English script' (he was also reinforcing the 'student contribution script'):

> The words sounded quite funny to some of the kids, but I thought I'd just test them out. And yes, they could guess 'paper' from the Cornish word, but the word for 'table' as I remember was quite strange and sounds quite funny in the mouth. And I think children ought to be able to do that: they ought to be able to laugh at that.

The reason for choosing to emphasize this particular aspect of the topic was grounded in the teacher's beliefs about the nature of his subject, and the ways in which students' access to knowledge of it might be facilitated most effectively:

> And I think, sometimes, language study can be seen as such serious and joyless subjects. And it's so revered that it becomes quite a stern body of knowledge in itself. And I try to break that down, because I think languages are quite funny things. And I think languages do sound funny. While I'm not encouraging children to be flippant at the way people speak – while I wouldn't encourage that – I just, you know, say that the study of language can be an interesting thing and often does raise a smile, particularly by the way certain words look, or when you look where they come from. And I like to try and instil that. So all I've got to do is use those words to open the lesson . . . and I

think presenting that to children in that way actually does relieve some of the anxiety. There's almost a sigh of relief, as if to say, 'Well, that's good then: we can look at it; we can have some fun with it, but we're not expected to know the answers!'

This extract shows how the teacher combined his knowledge of students (both his specific knowledge relating to the student who produced the dictionary and his general knowledge of student motivation) with his subject knowledge, and his knowledge of ways in which students' access to this knowledge can be facilitated (what Shulman (1986) describes as 'peda-gogical content knowledge'), in determining his course of action. The process by which he reached his final decision reveals an appreciation of the complex interplay between affective and motivational aspects of cog-nition: he believed that students' learning is facilitated most effectively when students are motivated, and that motivation can be enhanced through the creation of a positive affective climate.

Student responses to this lesson did not make overt reference to the fact that the introduction to the lesson was partly fashioned out of student input. However, they did suggest that the teacher has succeeded in legiti-mating certain aspects of the English student script that he referred to in his account of the lesson. The three students interviewed after this lesson all indicated that this phase of the lesson had been instrumental in achieving the teacher's intention of helping students to understand that dialect or other language, (a) although problematic is not rendered threatening by this, (b) can be amusing and (c) can be understood:

*S1:* He said, 'Can you get your . . .' And then he mentioned the words ['plumen' and 'paperyow'] . . . I was confused. I wondered what he was going on about.
*S2:* Didn't know what he was talking about. Thought he'd gone crazy.

Their tone, however, indicated amusement. A third student, referring to a later part of the same lesson, indicated that difficulty was not necessarily an impediment to enjoyment of dialect poems: '[Reading the dialect po-ems] was quite fun actually. A lot of people thought that the hardest one to read out was, like, the funniest.' Students 1 and 2 went on to contrast the experience of this lesson with modern language classes where they believed a similarly difficult activity was more than likely to give way to anxiety:

*S1:* Sometimes she [i.e. the French teacher] doesn't say what the word is. She has a book and she'll read the words out and won't tell you what some of them mean. A lot of us get lost . . .
*S2:* [It's worrying] because then she asks you to do questions about it and you don't know what she is on about.

*S1:* Mr A [i.e. the English teacher] wouldn't leave us. He's the sort of person who would tell us. And he might have given them to us [i.e. unfamiliar words] and waited a bit to see if we understood them, and then told us, like he did in that lesson.

Although these students clearly personalized their responses to the lesson with direct reference to the teacher, it is suggested that this response illustrates the way in which they were beginning to develop a view of English which was close to that held by the teacher in response to the scripts he had made available to them.

A second example, from the same unit of work, illustrates the particular value for students of integrating student input into the lesson, and exemplifies more clearly the mechanism of 'calibration'. The same teacher had asked the class to explain the difference between 'Standard English' and 'dialect'. During the lesson debrief the teacher described his intention as to make clear to students the distinction between these two terms, as a central predetermined objective of the lesson. A student provided what the teacher believed to be a particularly striking and apposite answer to this question, in the form of an elaborate metaphor, which the teacher then incorporated into the lesson through a process of reinforcement. There was evidence that the reinforcement had important implications for students' learning, in that it acted as a scaffold from which students developed their own representations. The reinforcement also had the effect of legitimizing this form of student response.

The truly interactional nature of this episode was illustrated at several points as it developed. Jim, the originator of the much valued metaphor, described its inception in terms of a response to teacher input. The teacher had previously given the class an explanation of the nature of and differences between standard English and dialect: 'Mr A told us, and I just got the idea off it.' He described the mechanism by which the transformation took place in terms that closely reflect Bruner and Haste's (1987) formulation of the concept of 'calibration':

I'm taking it [i.e. the teacher's explanation] in and pushing it out again in a different way . . . people put different things in their own terms, and you just adapt it to your own way. Somebody else might say, 'it's like the sea and the waves rise out of the sea and each wave's like a different dialect.' Maybe.

The process involved the student adjusting his internal representation of the teacher's explanation, in terms of his own existing patterns of understanding. It was a process of matching subjective understandings. Jim described the actual analogy he developed in the following terms:

We all have language, and everybody just branches off from it. And if we didn't all speak one language – sort of just a main middle stalk

or trunk, maybe – it would be like just a big wood, maybe. But we kept
it down to just one tree, with the branches . . . There's just one stalk
with the dialects branching off. And if they want to make a new word,
they come back to the branch and out sprouts another twig. And
maybe people get words off. Let's say Lancashire may say 'ain't',
Yorkshire got it off them, and said 'nain't', and maybe got it off them
and said 'main't', and 'gain't', and it all goes back to the same thing
maybe.

The teacher described his own in-lesson thinking and response to Jim's
input in the following terms, highlighting once again the complex array
of knowledge about the student, students in general, his aims as a teacher
and the subject:

I think you get the most rich work out of them [i.e. pupils] when they
are motivated; when they actually want to write or talk about something . . . I think . . . Jim is a good example of that because . . . normally
I think he's perhaps very frustrated by his perceived levels of achievement, because, as we said before, he has problems with his writing . . .
and I'm sure there's lots of negative feedback that he gets from various
adult areas [i.e. in school] that confirm that in his mind. So just that
one lesson where he came out with that wonderful example that I
told you about before [i.e. the tree analogy], when I took that out
and said, 'Right! I'm going to use that now. That's so good! I'm going
to use that in future because that's really sharpened my thinking.'
And because I made a big fuss over that, and particularly stressed it
in the lesson – kept going on about it, and I kept using it in front of
the class – you know, I could visibly see him perk up and start to puff
his chest out a bit and engage more in the lesson. So it was followed
then by other comments when, OK, he was trying to do the same
thing again, and perhaps never quite carried it off again. That doesn't
matter. The fact that he was engaged and he was contributing. And
all the way through the rest of the work his oral contribution was far
more significant [than usual] because, I think, he felt a little bit more
ownership. And I wrote it on the board, and some of them put it in
their books . . . And he could see his idea going down into people's
books.

He was describing his own experience of calibration, when he suggested
that the student's analogy had 'sharpened my thinking', thus suggesting
that the products of the student's initial calibration encapsulated the
teacher's subjective intention even more precisely than the teacher's own
original explanation. This illustrates well the continual and recursive nature
of calibration.

The impact of these events on other students was illustrated by a student who, in his recollection of the lesson, showed how he further transformed Jim's analogy into a form that was, presumably, more meaningful to him though still recognizably linked to Jim's original formulation. Further exemplifying the processes of scaffolding and calibration: 'He [i.e. Jim] said Standard English is like a horizontal line which people can come back to. And it's got lines going off it with different dialects. Standard English is what people come back to, to communicate with someone else from somewhere else.' The conceptualization of the distinction between Standard English and dialect can be seen to have gone through two trans-formations, each of which represented an example of calibration, whereby individual students developed their personal ways of understanding this particular item of knowledge that has been introduced by the teacher. The process was clearly aided by the teacher's efforts to highlight Jim's input and, thereby, to present Jim's behaviour as an appropriate script, and the substance of his input (i.e. as a metaphorical visualisation) as an appropriate way of interpreting the subject content. In this way the teacher's and Jim's efforts combined. Having had Jim's input highlighted and en-dorsed as appropriate, the student in this example used Jim's input as a 'scaffold' to develop his own representation of the content in the form of a similar, personalized metaphorical visualization.

A further aspect of scaffolding and script endorsement was illustrated in this example and that was the way in which the teacher facilitated learning and understanding through the use of student models. Students commonly reported, in the current study, that student models were preferred to teacher models because they facilitated the reaching of shared under-standings, and there were many examples, like the one cited above, of students finding their peers' transformations of teacher input facilitative of their own understanding and learning. This points to the particular value of the teacher actively employing student perceptions to mediate their learning objectives. This also underlines the socio-cultural aspect of calibration, as a mechanism which is facilitated by the extent to which interacting individuals share a field of reference. This suggests that the more successful the teacher is in focusing and facilitating effective pupil calibration, the more effective the teacher will be in facilitating effective pupil learning.

Another example of interactive teaching includes the English teacher's modification of her lesson plan to include an oral discussion and story telling exercise, in response to the apparent enthusiasm and motivation of her pupils when they brought in artefacts as a basis for story writing. A further example was provided by an English teacher who was teaching a unit on autobiography. She used a story about a member of her own family to illustrate the nature of autobiography. Her intention was then to get pupils to write their own autobiographies. However, she adjusted her plan when she found pupils keen to tell their own autobiographical stories, and devoted a considerable amount of the remainder of the lesson to the swapping of oral stories, using them to reinforce points she had made about the nature of autobiography. In history, pupil artefacts and oral stories served similar functions, with teachers being keen to incorporate them in this interactive way when time constraints permitted. An example of this was provided by the teacher who was teaching a unit on the nature of historical evidence. He was using a resource pack which contained a set of fictional evidence that could be used to deduce a chain of events. After working through this resource pack his plan was then to demonstrate to pupils the value of the principles of deduction in relation to an actual historical topic, in this case the Tollund Man story. In response to pupils' enthusiasm for and engagement with the fictional content and their direct requests, however, he permitted pupils to develop and discuss their own fictional detective stories before moving on to the Tollund Man task.

*Reactive teaching*

Purely reactive teaching occurred less commonly than the kind of inter-active teaching described above. The major difference between the in-teractive and reactive strategies was to do with the sequencing of the teacher's thought processes. When in purely interactive mode, the teach-er's first consideration was the range of learning objectives that he or she had developed prior to the lesson. In purely reactive mode the teacher's first consideration was his or her perceptions of student states or interests. Reactive teaching, therefore, describes the situation in which the teacher's choice of lesson objectives, lesson content and teaching strategy were determined by the teacher's perceptions of students' concerns or inter-ests. Another way of putting this is to see reactive teaching in terms of the teacher's willingness to negotiate with students about a wide range of decisions relating to teaching and learning experiences. A key point of interest here is that, in being reactive in this way, teachers sometimes created valuable learning situations which they had not foreseen and which they would have been unlikely to create had they started from the point of planned learning objectives.

A typical example of reactive teaching was provided by an English teacher who found herself in circumstances in which she felt constrained to offer her year 7 class a drama lesson, during a module on the topic of 'story': 'They usually have drama on a Monday, and I thought they'd probably lynch me if they hadn't got drama. So what could I do that's drama related, that will relate to story work as well?' The teacher's chosen so-lution was to select a poem which she believed 'lends itself to drama work'. It becomes clear that it was during the course of wrestling with these, to her, disparate objectives that she *discovered* a valuable teaching point. The drama exercise was thus transformed, in the view of the teacher, from a burdensome task that she would have preferred to have avoided, into a learning experience that she regretted being unable to develop later owing to the lack of availability of the drama room:

> Well, my first priority was to try and create a drama lesson – because they'd walked in yesterday and said, 'It's drama today, isn't it?' [Thereby confirming the teacher's expectation]. That was the main thing. And then it was to think of ways of actually getting across the idea of story telling with drama. Which is why I went for somebody telling the story and the others forming a little tableau. And it was just basically . . . a different way of tackling the idea [of story telling] . . . Ideally, it would have been nice to have gone back to the drama room today and been able to take that a stage further. But the drama room was in use.

The valuable learning point that the teacher believed to have emerged from the exercise was 'that one medium can be translated to a different one for a different purpose'.

There was a further emergent teaching point, which the teacher felt was not dealt with adequately. The teacher's description of the way in which the theme emerged in her thinking and the way in which it was ultimately, in her view, discarded were also indicative of the reactive mode:

> I walked into the drama room and thought, 'Oh gosh! This [poem] is [in the form of] a fairy tale, isn't it!' And I thought it might be interesting – the idea was there to get them to focus on what they thought a fairy tale was, and so to start off talking about a type of story. And then to get them to look at the poem, and then to say, 'How does this match with the idea [of a conventional fairy tale]?' But I could sense that they were so keen to be getting on with the drama that I actually forgot to come back to that point.

In this example the teacher's thinking and actions were explicitly directed towards the achievement of a close match between lesson activity and student interest. In addition to this, she was striving to scaffold students' activities in such a way as to advance their learning and understanding of English. Through this she illustrated a process that is very similar to that of 'calibration'. The intricate and recursive nature of the calibration process was reflected in the way in which she introduced the fairy tale theme, and then relinquished it in response to pupils' apparent keenness to 'get on with the drama'.

This example shows the way in which reactive teaching could sometimes lead to the development of teaching and learning opportunities that were unforeseen by the teacher. Confirmation of some of the teacher's perceptions of learning opportunities was provided in the post-lesson student interviews. The students interviewed were mostly concerned with their enjoyment of the dramatic activity, the complexities of transforming the poem into a performance and the way in which the lesson had raised their awareness of the structural features of fairy tale form. This girl emphasized the structural aspects of fairy tale:

> [The lesson was about] acting, thinking what a fairy tale was. Thinking what they're doing in the fairy tale . . . Usually they have a happy ending, occasionally they don't, but a lot of the time they do. There's usually nice characters and horrible characters . . . I think I knew about them [i.e. the characteristics of fairy tales], but I hadn't thought about them [before this lesson].

This boy described the way in which his group generated a method of dramatic characterization by introducing events which were not in the original poem:

*S:* We put at the beginning that she was doing all the work for the husband, like getting cups of tea, sewing and stuff like that . . .
*I:* That was what you introduced, was it?
*S:* Yeah.
*I:* What was in the original?
*S:* It just said [in the poem] that no one's on her side, and she couldn't stand anything that he did, so she ran away . . .
*I:* So you actually made that up: her being bossed around. Why was that?
*S:* To make out that the husband was horrible.

In stating that his group had managed to generate solutions to the problems of transferring a story from one medium to another, this student indicated that the task had been successfully scaffolded by the teacher through her division of the students into groups and her efforts in setting up the task (i.e. instructions to student and choice of poem). As a result of this scaffolding these students engaged in the kind of thinking that the teacher believed the activities she set would engender.

Another example of reactive teaching was provided by an English teacher who was asked by pupils if they could produce a 'radio play' using a cassette recorder. Although the unit she was teaching was concerned with the play form, she had not planned for this, preferring to have the pupils simply perform their plays to the class. However, she permitted the group to develop their play as a sound play only, and then went on to use what they produced as a resource to explore with the group as a whole the particular differences between sound-only drama and visual drama. These were aspects of the topic that she had not planned to address, but as a result of this experience she recognized their significance.

It can be seen that there were important differences between the interactive and reactive modes, which can be related to differences in the form and use of *scripts, scaffolding* and *calibration*. In reactive mode student influence was more dominant. Student scripts, in reactive mode, would appear to have been more negotiable than they are in interactive mode, and likely to give students influence over areas of teacher decision-making that in the interactive mode were the preserve of the teachers alone, such as the generation of lesson objectives. Scaffolding was more likely to involve student collaboration that was not mediated by teachers in the reactive mode (e.g. when students in the drama lesson solve the characterization problem when transforming a poem into a drama). In terms of calibration, it would seem that in the interactive mode the teachers defined the focus for student calibration and filtered out unwanted foci in order to meet objectives (e.g. when the teacher highlighted Jim's representation of the nature of Standard English). In reactive mode teachers were less in control of the foci of students' calibrations, because they were less in control of learning objectives.

## The interactive–reactive continuum

The essential difference between reactive and interactive teaching centred on the extent to which teachers allowed lesson activity to be determined by their perceptions of student states or interests and the manner in which they allowed this to proceed. In practice, for a great deal of the time teachers in the present study employed teaching approaches that combined interactive and reactive elements, with lessons being directed towards clear learning objectives but also containing spaces for pupils to develop their own lines of interest. Thus reactive and interactive teaching existed within a broader context of other teaching approaches, being employed as and when conditions seemed appropriate to the teachers concerned. This was exemplified when teachers structured their lessons to meet preset objectives, while allowing and often encouraging pupils to present their own interests and concerns, in the ways described under the heading of 'interactive teaching'. Within this context teachers would sometimes permit what might be termed pupil deviations, with a view to seeing where they led. On occasions, where the deviation was seen to be fruitful, this would be permitted to continue. Most often, however, the deviation was permitted to continue for a limited period, at the end of which the teacher would steer the class back to the original path. Thus a lesson which was dealing with the decline of the Roman Empire and, in particular, the degeneration in the quality of the Roman army, at one point was diverted into a discussion of the nature of Roman weaponry, prompted by a pupil's question about one of the illustrations in a textbook that was being used. Although this was not directly related to the focus of the lesson that the teacher had planned, he allowed the deviation to continue, in the form of a class discussion, for some time, without seeing any historical relevance in the discussion, but acknowledging the value of allowing pupils to express interest and enthusiasm. As the discussion developed the teacher recognized that some pupils were beginning to interrogate the illustration as a source of evidence, and to point out that its reliability might be suspect because its relationship to primary sources was not evident. The teacher finally brought the discussion to a close by highlighting this historical point, and then directed the pupils back towards the original focus of the lesson.

There were various factors influencing the employment of interactive or reactive approaches. Some of these differences could be related to individual differences between teachers, while others were related to the teachers' perceptions of specific conditions in which they were teaching. Teachers who engaged in detailed preactive planning tended to be less willing to depart from their planned lesson contents than those whose planning was less detailed. Similarly, where lesson content was perceived to require careful pre-planning, teaching tended to the interactive rather than reactive. This latter point is illustrated well by the history teachers in this study, who unanimously interpreted the KS3 history curriculum as requiring the delivery of a high degree of factual content. This meant that these teachers found less opportunity for reactive teaching than some of them would have liked, because they felt constrained by the limited time available to them to maximize their coverage of curriculum content. This meant that often they felt constrained to engage in a transmission style of teaching, which, generally, they believed to be weak in terms of its ability to advance student understanding or learning, but an efficient method for achieving maximal coverage of content. Where this happened it tended to be the case that only those students who were judged to be 'more able' and in need of extension tasks were given opportunities to develop areas of personal interest.

### Conclusions and hypotheses

An important area that the research has illuminated is that of teacher–student 'bi-directionality'. We have presented here an account of teaching and learning which illuminates the *interdependence* of teacher and student influence. On the basis of this study it would seem that teachers are very alert to what they see as the desirability of being open to pupil influence and the need to incorporate pupil influence in their classroom teaching, though they vary in the degree to which they do this and in the methods they use in order to do this in different circumstances. The content of student concerns most relevant to this process would appear to be students' existing knowledge and understanding, and their preferred and most available cognitive strategies for developing and extending understanding and knowledge.

If our observations about bi-directionality are sustainable, they will have important implications for the ways in which we think about teaching methods. The present study would suggest that teachers and pupils believe that effective teaching occurs when the teaching strategy is selected with *full* regard to the *specific* circumstances and conditions in which the teaching is to take place. Included in the range of circumstances and conditions is a primary regard for students' concerns, perceptions and learning requirements, along with the teachers' knowledge of appropriate learning activities, teaching methods and learning outcomes.

There are times, however, when other contextual factors, such as the limitations imposed by the structure and content of the National Curriculum, are seen to conflict with purely pedagogical concerns. A strategy is rendered effective for students when it is experienced as fitting with their specific learning requirements, while for teachers there appears to be a wider spectrum of criteria, not all of which are concerned with student learning outcomes. It is for this reason that the concept of a *continuum* of teaching strategies would appear to be important to our understanding of effective teaching. Some teachers appear to be able to move back and forth along this continuum, going from transmission modes through interactive–reactive modes and towards ever more student-centred approaches, and back again. In fact, it can be hypothesized that their belief in their degree of overall effectiveness is related to their ability and willingness to move back and forth along this continuum in response to their perceptions of the learning requirements of their students and other contextual factors.

This hypothesis gains strength from what we have reported about some of the differences between teacher and pupil perceptions and difference among pupil perceptions. In the next chapter it will be shown that pupils perceived to be at different levels of the ability hierarchy sometimes have different and even conflicting learning requirements. The teacher's attempts to meet one or other of these different requirements *alone*, in these circumstances, lead to a failure to meet the requirements of the other. This underlines the potential dangers inherent in thinking about teaching strategies in terms of good and bad dichotomies. Effective teaching, it would seem, is more likely to depend on the teacher's mastery of a wide range of strategies (e.g. from transmission to self-direction) and, importantly, the ability to evaluate circumstances that render the application of a particular strategy appropriate to student requirements. Sometimes a global strategy for whole groups will be appropriate, and may require the teacher to engage in a transmission style; at other times more student-directed approaches will be appropriate. These kinds of decisions depend on the teacher's understanding of the active role that students need to play in the learning process and the benefits that are to be derived from teacher–student consultation and collaboration, but also on the many other factors of which teachers need to take account.

These findings would suggest that there are times when the teacher's willingness to allow students the space to engage with learning activities in their preferred ways, and even to have influence on the selection of objectives, facilitates what teachers and students believe to be effective learning. This would further indicate that effective teaching may well involve a degree of teacher-regulated power sharing in classrooms. In these circumstances, it might be tentatively suggested, the teacher's success in terms of student learning outcomes is likely to be dependent on the skill with which he or she makes judgements about how much power to share, in which areas and when.

# 7 / Catering for individual differences between pupils

In Chapters 4 to 6 we have described and analysed some of the ways in which teachers and pupils interact to produce what they believe to be effective teaching and learning. In particular we have shown how, in the accounts of both teachers and pupils, great importance is attached to ways in which teachers respond to pupil concerns. We now take another step forward, by moving from this account of how teachers respond to pupils in general, to how teachers in this study construed and responded to individual differences among their pupils. In the course of this chapter we will consider some of the ways in which teachers in our study thought about the differences between the pupils in their mixed ability classes. We will also see how some of this knowledge fed into their decision-making processes when they taught. The chapter is divided into three main sections.

1 *Teachers' perceptions of individual differences:* this section focuses on teachers' use of constructs that can be summarized under the headings of ability, behaviour and motivation and personal attributes.
2 *The typing of pupils:* this section describes the processes through which teachers developed stabilized conceptions of pupils' academic and behavioural profiles and assigned to them roles and identities.
3 *Teachers' responses to individual differences:* this section deals with the ways in which teachers went about meeting pupils' individual learning needs, and focuses in particular on teachers' concerns about pupils with learning difficulties and pupils perceived to have high academic ability; it will be shown how teachers cope with these circumstances through the use of individualized measures and group methods.

## Teachers' perceptions of individual differences

When the teachers in this study were asked to talk about what they saw as important similarities and differences between the pupils they taught there was a surprising degree of commonality in the constructs employed by different teachers. An exercise that all teachers were asked to do at the beginning of each unit was to prepare an annotated list of all the pupils in the class to be taught. They were asked to provide a one-line comment for each pupil giving any information that they thought to be important from a teaching point of view.

Teachers who were asked to do this in the very early weeks (up to week 7) of year 7 found it difficult to comment on every pupil, on the grounds that at this stage they were often unable to put names to faces. In these circumstances the teachers tended to comment on pupils whom they perceived to be in some sense exceptional. This is illustrated through reference to an English teacher's annotated list, which contains comments for only seven out of a class of 30 pupils (15 boys, 15 girls):

Pupil 10 boy: 12 going on 70 – accurate but appalling presentation.
Pupil 11 boy: Very good [academically].
Pupil 17 girl: Social misfit – can make or break mood of class.
Pupil 19 girl: With pupil 17. Burst into tears when split up from friends. Sulked. Very moody. Every member of staff picked her out in the first week.
Pupil 22 girl: Very poor [academically], but trying. Candidate for SEN withdrawal.
Pupil 27 boy: Good. Organizational skills are good.
Pupil 28 boy: Weak. Poor punctuation.

The constructs employed are all evaluative. This teacher picks out pupils: who are academically weak or strong; whose presentational skills are poor; who are socially deviant and potentially disruptive. She also mentions motivation (pupil 22). The reference to pupil 10 as being '12 going on 70' is curious, and almost a verbatim echo of a comment made by an English teacher from another school in the study, who described a boy as '12 going on 40: a splendid character'. This comment shows the importance teachers attach to idiosyncracies or eccentricities of pupil personality. The underlying concern of this teacher is to identify pupils who will affect the ease or difficulty of the teaching task. Thus academic concerns focus on pupils' skills or lack of skills, implying the need to address particular learning targets (e.g. presentational skills, spelling), and explicitly referring to a pupil who will probably need learning support provision. Behavioural observations reveal concerns about the effects of behaviour on the class group and non-cooperation (i.e. moodiness and sulking), indicating an alertness to possible management and discipline problems.

Across all the teacher-annotated class lists three major categories of individual differences emerge:

1 Differences relating to pupil ability, including references to their academic performance and potential.
2 Differences relating to pupil behaviour and motivation, including imputations of deviance, evidence and/or suspicions of disruptive tendencies and pupil moodiness.
3 Differences relating to pupils' personal attributes, including their physical, interactional and psychological characteristics.

We will now look at these categories in greater detail to draw out their apparent importance to teachers.

### Differences relating to pupil ability

References to pupil ability are less pervasive in the unit 1 lists than in later unit lists. Teachers' comments on this subject often combine a global observation about a pupil's general ability level with a reference to the pupil's performance of specific skills. For example:

Low ability. Quite weak. Spelling problems. Sparce writing. Orally lively.

Very, very bright – this side of gifted. Enormous problems with writing and presentation.

Not over bright . . . terrible speller.

The global comments tend to categorize pupils as 'average', 'very good', 'weak' or 'bright'. English teachers also sometimes use the concept of 'talent' or 'flair', e.g. 'Intelligent, sensitive girl who enjoys life and is talented with words.' Both English and history teachers talk in terms of pupils' levels of understanding, e.g. 'Understanding weak. Prefers oral structure.' One history teacher provides the following statement that he applies to 11 of the 31 pupils in his class: 'Those who seem to show a good understanding of work done so far in history.' References to pupils' skills refer mostly to writing (content and presentation), reading and spelling, with some attention to talking:

SN [i.e. pupil with special educational needs], weak writer, but an able talker.

Slight spelling problems . . . difficulty with handwriting.

Written work sometimes inaccurate; spelling poor.

Oracy not so good; good on paper.

Low achiever. Spelling, reading and writing need support.

There are also references to the pace at which pupils complete work, e.g. 'Slow worker, potentially weak.'

A further category of concern, which is often related to teachers' notions of ability, is that of pupil 'progress'. While 'progress' is not technically an aspect of ability, teachers seem to use the terms in very similar ways. Both the child who is perceived to have high ability and the child who is 'making good progress' are seen by teachers as being non-problematic, in that the clasroom performance of both these pupil types indicates that they are able to take advantage of the classroom learning opportunities that the teacher is providing. Where children are perceived to be underachieving or to have learning difficulties, these problems are translated into a teaching task:

> Thomas has problems . . . learning problems . . . I would say his reading age is seven, something like that . . . So basically he can't read the books we've got. But more and more I'm beginning to think that he's in that awful situation where he . . . does understand a lot . . . He listens well in class and understands well . . . I'm wondering if sometimes he does get bored, because he isn't given enough to do that he can do on his own that is specific enough for him.

Here the problem is one of matching resources to perceived need. The teacher's concern with the difficulties in meeting this boy's needs sheds light on why teachers often seem to place a high value on pupils who are 'bright' or who make 'steady progress', and who, by definition, do not make undue demands on available resources. This point is further underlined by this same teacher's concern about pupils whose progress is too rapid; such pupils also place a strain on teacher resources, particularly when they are being taught in mixed ability settings where the spread of ability is perceived to be wide:

> I find with this group that there are children like [she names seven children she regards as being of high ability and who make good progress] who I need to make sure I've got plenty of work up my sleeve for them. This is what I find the most difficult thing, because I've got Thomas [see above] at one end and I've got these at the other.

This brings us back to where we started this section and gives us insight into why these teachers paid such close attention in their early encounters with their classes to pupils who fall into extreme categories and, therefore, might prove to be particularly demanding: this applies to children with learning and behavioural difficulties as well as pupils who are perceived to be particularly 'bright'.

The main sources of teachers' knowledge of pupils' ability comes from teachers' observation of pupils' classroom performance in oral question and answer situations, as well as knowledge of their performance in specific tasks, such as in reading aloud or, in particular, in their written work:

Promising: wrote immediately in paragraphs.

Absolutely super – immediately extended his writing.

Continues to shine . . . brill story the other day.

Last piece of written work was controlled and mature.

Only one teacher refers to a single child's performance on a standardized test: '[He's] out [i.e. withdrawn from mainstream] of English for extra English: did poorly on reading test.'

For the most part these teachers seem to have relied on their own first-hand judgements of pupils based on their observation of pupil behaviour and their judgement of work products.

### Differences relating to pupil behaviour and motivation

Pupil behaviour and motivation were major preoccupations of the teachers in this study. Initial written comments on pupils showed that teachers were able to make assessments of pupils' motivational levels quite early in their aquaintance with them. For example, from unit 1:

Interested and enthusiastic.

Needs gentle nudging.

Poorly motivated.

Lazy.

Hard working.

Desperately keen.

Once again, the source of data on which these judgements are based, when mentioned, is teachers' first-hand experience of pupils in the class-room situation:

Badly motivated. Doesn't do homework. Fiddles. Badly organized. Messy work. Can be diligent.

Tries: offers ideas orally.

Lazy. Tries to get away with doing nothing [in class].

These teachers were particularly concerned with pupil talk. It is important to note, however, that there are subtle variations between different types of talk. There is undesirable talk:

Talkative and silly at times.

Can be talkative.

She's a real chatterbox.

There is desirable talk:

Orally lively.

Good orally.

Weak writer, but able talker!

There is deficient talk:

Very quiet. Needs to participate more.

Written work is developing but still reticent in discussion.

Pupils' oral behaviour was used as an important factor in teachers' responses to their pupils. It was used to make judgements about cognitive ability, motivation and behaviour, and pupil personality. This again underlines the importance that teachers attached to their first-hand experience of pupils.

As in the case of teachers' attributions of pupil ability, teachers' remarks about pupils' motivational and behavioural characteristics are often put in relation to the demands these characteristics make on teachers' workload:

Poorly motivated – needs cajoling.

Occasional lapses: needs to be stimulated.

This often relates to implications for classroom management:

Still highly motivated – but too excitable at times. Can go off task.

Immature. Doesn't always pay attention. Flighty (poor concentration). Doesn't find it easy to settle.

By contrast to the negative implications of low motivation for classroom management, the well-motivated pupil can be an aid to effective management:

Very able, highly motivated. A great asset!

Contributes well.

This quality can even compensate for other individual pupil deficits: 'She's orally excellent. She's quite bright, but her written work sort of doesn't live up to expectations sometimes. Maybe she doesn't concentrate enough because she talks too much. But she's good to have in the class, though. She's full of all sorts of ideas.' In these circumstances the teachers tended to find well motivated, orally contributing pupils helpful in maintaining the pace and flow of lessons, by enabling teachers to engage in interactive forms of teaching, often structured around question and answer situations. Pupils who can be relied upon to make apposite oral interjections were welcomed for the way in which their contributions helped to vary the stimulus in lessons, by preventing lessons from being dominated by too much teacher talk. Teachers also referred to the mediating effects of pupil contributions, which often helped other pupils to understand teachers' input by translating it into pupil friendly language. Again, however, teachers indicated that there is an optimum level of motivation/participation, which could become dysfunctional not only when pupils fail to reach it, but also when pupils exceed it:

Very (over?) enthusiastic. Can get too excited.

Enthusiastic. Sometimes too enthusiastic.

Still highly motivated – but too excitable at times. Can go off task.

In these circumstances pupils pose a threat to good order in the class-room, thereby creating management difficulties for teachers.

Pupils' oral participation also provides teachers with data about pupils' levels of understanding and indicates their rates of progress. Pupils who are orally reticent, therefore, pose problems for teachers in that it is not always obvious when they need help: 'Very quiet. Not sure would ask if problem.' Again, pupils who are orally confident – even those with sup-posed learning difficulties (which are almost entirely determined in relation to literacy skills) – can facilitate teacher performance by requesting help, or by exhibiting their need for help in the oral question and answer situations of the type that many of these teachers employed in order to monitor the effectiveness of their teaching, and to gauge pupil progress and understanding.

Teachers' comments on pupils' inappropriate behaviour tended to re-flect their powerful concerns with classroom management issues. Certain forms of pupil behaviour gained their significance for teachers from the ways in which they related to other concerns. One major area of concern was the need to maintain a desirable rate of progress through the cur-riculum, so that lessons met the criterion of having 'covered' an appropriate portion of the syllabus. A second related area of concern was the need for pupils to be appropriately occupied. This was often described in terms of 'on task' behaviour: 'Too excitable at times. Can go off task.' This is also reflected in the interview data, which show that, for these teachers, pupils' willingness to apply themselves to classroom tasks was often seen as a redeeming feature, even in the face of other less desirable traits, such as perceived lack of ability and/or a tendency to over-talkativeness:

[He] works well most of the time. He is sometimes a bit of a chatterbox. [His] work's nothing outstanding, but he gets on with it.

He's the sort of macho man of the class – he works quite well. Nothing outstanding, but he gets his head down.

She's not over-bright, but she does get on with it, in her own way.

On the other hand, teachers identified pupils and pupil behaviours which threatened the orderly running of the classroom (see above):

Makes trouble for others while staying out of it herself.

Immature: doesn't always pay attention.

Common among undesirable behaviours were talking at times deemed inappropriate by the teacher, engaging in activities that distracted other pupils from their work and failing to keep on task as a result of active engagement in alternative behaviour, inactivity or 'day dreaming'. The exhibition of these characteristics, however, was less important to teachers than their manageability. Thus, pupils could possess these characteristics, but would only be a cause for concern if the teacher felt unable to manage the consequences of the behaviour: 'Can be silly. Easily led. Not a problem.' In this case the pupil's willingness to 'take a telling' meant that his behaviour was not perceived as a problem. On the other hand, a pupil who was prone to tantrum behaviour was seen as a major threat to classroom discipline, because the teacher felt unable to influence her behaviour: 'Social misfit – can make or break the mood of class.' This teacher's underlying concern was clearly the effect that this pupil had on the rest of the class. Again, the important issue here for teachers appeared to be the degree to which pupils' behavioural characteristics aided or hindered them in their efforts to manage the classroom situation.

## Differences relating to pupils' personal attributes

A third category of difference identified by the teachers in this study was composed of a wide ranging set of characteristics that we have loosely termed 'personal attributes'. These are stated in terms of individual and sometimes idiosyncratic qualities of pupils, encapsulating matters of temperament and personality, as well as social and psychological characteristics. While some of these characteristics overlap with issues of ability, behaviour and motivation, they are treated separately from these because the teachers themselves used them, at times, in isolation from these other characteristics. Overlapping characteristics included references to pupils'

• levels of personal confidence;
• levels of self-discipline/self-reliance;

- maturity;
- organizational skills.

A sub-category of characteristics refers to pupils' 'social problems', such as a pupil's difficulties within the family: 'This child needs support, he is socially preoccupied with family problems.' In this case, for example, the teacher's concern was with the child's need for counselling.

A second sub-category was composed of teachers' judgements about pupils' general personality characteristics and whether they found the pupils likeable or not. An important aspect of these judgements was often whether or not teachers felt that they 'understood' pupils. Teachers who used this term sometimes expressed a sense of discomfort when they came across a pupil whom they were not able to make definitive judgements about.

A related characteristic is that of teacher 'interest'. Certain pupils were described as 'interesting', in relation to their apparent cognitive characteristics, their personal styles in terms of self-presentation, their sense of humour or their manner of engagement in the classroom experience. By contrast, there was a small group of pupils who did not excite teacher interest, and as a consequence attracted sometimes relatively dismissive comments, as these contrasting comments from the same teacher illustrate:

Pupil 1: Gorgeous – delightful!

Pupil 2: Nice. Very quiet. Very straightforward and solid type of person.

Relatively negative comments occur sometimes in spite of the possession of other positive qualities, such as: 'Very quiet, wishy washy sort of girl. Near the top of the lower [ability] band.'

A third sub-category of comment under the heading of personal attributes is that of physical appearance. This tends, almost exclusively, to occur in the initial stages of the teachers' acquaintance with the group. Sometimes reference to physical appearance has no obvious significance attached to it, other than it being the only comment attached to the child: 'Little West Indian girl.' At other times, the reference to physical type seems to be part of an overall archetype, with connotations of appeal or otherwise for the teacher:

Very bright – aristocratic – blonde – neat and powerful personality.

Quiet little mouse, hard working, very pretty.

Limited but amiable – slow, fattish with little imagination.

Small, blond, cheeky – bright – a favourite!

Tall, blond, quiet strong type – appropriate use of imagery in his writing emerging.

*Key issues in teachers' notions of difference*

Teachers seem to be expressing a number of different concerns when they make judgements about differences among their pupils. These concerns include:

- the need to make judgements about pupils' abilities in order to plan appropriately differentiated work for whole class and individuals;
- making judgements about pupil performance and behaviour in relation to classroom process, in order to judge the degree to which pupils can be relied upon to aid or hinder the teacher in the management of lessons and assessment of progress (such as identifying pupils who can be relied upon to make effective contributions to lessons, or identifying pupils who do not alert the teacher to their needs or state of understanding);
- identifying pupils whose behavioural characteristics require particular attention in relation to the design of learning tasks and the planning of lesson activities;
- identifying pupils whose personal characteristics are a source of personal interest or stimulation to teachers.

These teachers seemed to be generally preoccupied with differences between pupils that related to their need to manage the classroom process. Therefore, they tended to indicate a preference for pupils who displayed their abilities clearly and consistently within the range of the majority of pupils within the class being taught. The degree to which pupils made their needs and abilities visible and accessible to teachers in the whole-class situation was an important management consideration; hence the concern with pupils who appeared to be 'too quiet' or 'reserved', and the general preference for outgoing and orally active pupils. This was regardless of pupils' literacy skills, and in spite of the fact that literacy skills tended to be the main reference point for comments about pupils' overall ability levels within a given subject. Pupils who fall outside the general ability range for the class, either above or below, tend to be perceived as problematic, from pedagogic and organizational viewpoints. There was also a sense, however, in which teachers made judgements about pupils on the basis of what appeared to be their own needs for stimulation and interest arousal: they simply liked certain pupils because they found them personally appealing and, therefore, contributory to a pleasant working context in the classroom.

An important unifying feature, therefore, underlying the judgements these teachers made about pupil differences, seems to have been their interest in (a) maintaining a classroom situation that was manageable from a teaching and organizational point of view, in such a way that all pupils' learning needs were met, and (b) having a stimulating and congenial working environment.

## The typing of pupils

This section describes briefly the processes through which teachers developed stabilized conceptions of certain pupils' academic and behavioural profiles and assigned to them roles and identities. The process bears many similarities to that described by Hargreaves *et al.* (1975) in their study of deviance in classrooms.

First, it is notable that teachers in this study, when making judgements about pupils, tended to focus on different characteristics for different pupils. Thus, while some pupils were described in terms of their ability, behaviour and personality, some pupils were referred to in relation to only one or two of these characteristics. In interviews this emphasis was confirmed, particularly in the case of pupils who were seen to exhibit extremes of ability or behaviour. The overwhelming majority of pupils were given attributions relating to their ability, of the 'weak', 'able', 'average' or 'gifted' variety. In certain cases pupils had specific roles attributed to them, such as 'class clown' or 'mother hen'. Signs of the rigidity of their typing were also detected in some extreme cases, where it was indicated that teachers were resistant to changes in pupil behaviour that might undermine the identity that had been attributed:

Social misfit – can make or break the mood of class (unit 1).

Very severe social and academic problems. She has to be treated with kid gloves (unit 2).

What's changed??? Getting better but still has her moments. Can be moody and uncooperative (unit 3).

Thus even when this child's behaviour appears to have improved this is still the only aspect that the teacher chooses to make a comment about. The fact that she ceases to be continually difficult is not as significant as the fact that she still behaves in this manner occasionally. This is indicative of a stabilized deviant identity (Hargreaves *et al.* 1975).

Having said this, teachers in this study were less likely to indicate stabilized attributions of deviance, tending to reserve judgement on this issue throughout year 7, and to maintain a speculative stance on this issue. This was not the case with attributions of extremes of ability and other characteristics, however. Teachers in this study made clear and early attributions about *extremes* of ability. Evidence from interviews, as well as written comments, indicates that such attributions tended to be made relatively early in teachers' relationships with pupils: certainly within the first term, and probably in the very early part of the first term. It is notable, for example, that teachers who were interviewed and required to provide notes on their pupils early in the first term (i.e. within the first seven weeks) could often only make comments about pupils who 'stood out' in terms of high or low ability. There was a tendency for comments made in the first term to focus on issues other than ability, for most pupils, though by the end of the second term all teachers were able to express fairly clear opinions about the ability levels of virtually all of their pupils. These attributions then remained, for the most part, stable for the rest of the year, with only a very few pupils being subjects for speculation. Key indicators of ability were seen to be pupils' early performance in literacy tasks and the quality of their oral contributions in whole-class situations. It was rare for these initial impressions to be overturned or significantly changed. Pupil performances that challenged these initial views tended to be seen as aberrant.

### Teachers' responses to individual differences

This section deals with the ways in which teachers in this study went about meeting pupils' individual learning needs, and focuses in particular on teachers' concerns about pupils with learning difficulties and pupils perceived to have high academic ability; it will be shown how teachers coped with these circumstances through the use of individualized measures and group methods. The following key points emerge from our analysis.

- All the teachers in this study devoted a considerable amount of their time to whole-class teaching.
- A major concern of teachers in these circumstances was to ensure that pupils of perceived low ability would not be excluded from the learning process. Measures taken to achieve this included:
  (a) an emphasis on oral explanation (several teachers put a particular emphasis on the mediating function of pupils' oral responses, which they often saw as a way of 'translating' teaching material into pupil speak);
  (b) story telling;
  (c) oral question and answer sessions, with questions individually tailored to particular pupils' perceived ability levels;
  (d) multiple exemplification;
  (e) the use of pictorial and diagrammatic stimuli;
  (f) group reading sessions led by the teacher or most competent pupil readers;
  (g) drama and role play;
  (h) the use of highly structured written tasks to help pupils with writing difficulties.
- Specific measures taken to help pupils with particular difficulties, including one-to-one work involving the teacher or a learning support assistant, or the use of peer tutors.

- Extension work for pupils of perceived high ability was also provided in some cases.
- Within the whole-class structure groupwork was sometimes used, most often involving doing the same tasks. The groups were selected by teachers or self-selected depending on the teachers' perceptions of the task. Teachers constructed mixed ability groups where the task was felt to be particularly demanding for 'weaker' pupils; they selected groups on social and behavioural grounds when the task was perceived to create scope for disruption; all teachers tended to require groups to be mixed in terms of gender.
- Teachers made increasing use of differentiated tasks and materials as time went by and their perceptions of pupil differences became stabilized.
- A major means by which teachers attempted to respond to pupil needs in the whole-class situation was the use of reactive and interactive teaching strategies (see Chapter 6). This involved incorporating what teachers perceived to be pupil concerns and orientations in their planning and execution of lessons. These processes often depended on teachers' perceptions of pupils' concerns gleaned from classroom interactions, or from pupils who made direct requests and inputs. This was rarely the result of direct or systematic consultation, with the resulting tendency that the most vocal and active pupils dominated the agenda. Thus teachers tended to judge the feeling of the whole class on the basis of the output of the most vocal and active minority, who performed the role of a 'steering group' (Dahllof and Lundgren 1970). Pupils by and large, however, seemed to accept this without complaint.

Generally speaking the teachers' methods of catering for individuals were appreciated by the vast majority of pupils, including those perceived by their teachers to be academically weak. Pupils teachers saw as 'bright', however, sometimes found the pacing of lessons too slow. They also complained that the high degree of structure and the use of multiple examples were frustrating because they were felt to interfere with these pupils' desire to exercise their personal creativity and individuality. For example, there was general agreement between teachers and pupils about the value of the teacher reading aloud. They agreed that this often aided pupil comprehension by helping them to circumvent possible decoding difficulties, and their use of expression also helped to elucidate meaning. Many pupils described the way in which teachers' reading provided them with a model that enabled them to make greater sense of a text when, later, they came to read it themselves. In this situation each subsequent reading added to the foundation of understanding fostered by the teacher's initial reading. During the teacher's reading many pupils formulated impressions that were later filled out by their own readings. Some pupils, however, including some of those in the 'more able' category, described this practice as irritating, and complained that it interfered with their personal interpretations and cognitive representations of a text. Similarly, teachers' use of multiple exemplifications, in whatever form, came in for criticism from these pupils, who complained at the redundancy of much of it for them.

A second subset of pupils consisted of those who had learning difficulties in the fields of writing (in particular) and/or reading. Many of these pupils had well-developed oral and cognitive skills, but were frustrated by the use of literacy skills as instruments of learning. Consequently, where teachers required pupils to demonstrate understanding, knowledge or cognitive skills through the use of reading or, in particular, writing skills, these pupils were foiled. While their more literate counterparts often spoke about the cognitive aspects of such lessons, with little or no reference to literacy skills, the pupils with literacy difficulties focused entirely on the literacy requirements of the same lessons. For these pupils every lesson that involved written work was a lesson *dominated* by written work. This applied not only to those pupils whom teachers believed to have formal learning difficulties, but related, in different degrees, to pupils outside this group whose skills proved inadequate to the tasks presented.

It is interesting to note that all the teachers in this study showed an awareness of this problem. However, while they employed many varied and sophisticated strategies for dealing with reading problems, they showed less confidence in their approach to writing problems. Pupils and teachers agreed on the efficacy of teaching strategies aimed at helping pupils with reading difficulties, such as:

- teacher reading aloud;
- paired reading;
- shared reading;
- teacher (learning support assistant or more competent pupil) highlighting salient points of text).

There were only isolated examples of pupils claiming to be helped by teachers with their writing. When this occurred it often took one of three forms:

- the teacher rehearsed orally the writing that was to be done;
- the teacher provided a written structure on the blackboard on which pupils were required to model their writing;
- the teacher (pupil or learning support assistant) acted as scribe while the pupil dictated what was to be written.

Pupil coping strategies included forms of informal peer tutoring. This sometimes involved straightforward copying, with minor modifications, of a peer's work. One pupil had a personal strategy that he described in terms of 'sensing'. This took the form of anticipating when blackboard notes prepared by the teacher would be required to be transcribed by pupils. When he 'sensed' that this was likely to be the case he began transcribing the notes as the teacher prepared them. This enabled him to avoid the problem of 'falling behind', which was a major fear and pre-occupation of this and other pupils with writing and learning difficulties. In this pupil's case the fear of falling behind was particularly associated with the confusion he experienced when required to deal with large passages of text, for reading and/or transcription.

The problems associated with the role of literacy skills in learning are important, and represent a set of concerns shared by teachers and pupils. Teachers of both history and English were aware of the literacy difficulties faced by some pupils. Some of these teachers were concerned about the ways in which their own professional and academic socialization had an adverse effect on their treatment of this issue, leading them to place an unnecessary reliance on literacy as a learning medium. The following quotation from a history teacher illustrates the way in which some teachers believed that the overuse of literacy skills created barriers to pupil learning:

> I'm not sure they've understood the issue [i.e. the focus of the lesson in terms of the learning objectives she had set] . . . And maybe I shouldn't have bothered about any written work at all. I mean, I've got a bit of a hang up about written work. I suppose because I started my teaching career in the days of O level . . . I find it quite difficult to say: hang on a minute, there's no need for them to have a written record of this. You know, we could have just spent the whole lesson – on reflection now – just doing it through role play, and understanding the issue.

A further dimension to the problem identified by this teacher relates to the way in which teachers in this study believed that the National Curriculum, through its assessment arrangements and the weight of content in the history, was likely to push them further away from teaching approaches that were flexible enough to compensate for the difficulties referred to here. The pressure to achieve 'coverage' of the syllabus often seems to have led teachers to a greater reliance on directive and literacy-based approaches than they would have preferred.


## Conclusions

This chapter has briefly described some of the key ways in which teachers in this study construed and responded to individual differences between their pupils. A major theme here is that these teachers' judgements and responses were informed by their concerns about the management of the classroom situation, the need to maintain an adequate rate of progress through the curriculum and their desire to maintain a relatively congenial working environment. Teachers' concerns about the personal and social characteristics of their pupils are consonant with findings reported elsewhere in this book, which show the importance both teachers and pupils attach to the social climate of the classroom and how this relates to the provision of learning opportunities (see also Cooper and McIntyre 1993, 1994a,b).

This study confirms the findings of previous studies in indicating that a generalized typing of pupils in terms of 'ability' or 'academic progress' plays an important part in secondary school teachers' professional craft knowledge. It is clear that the teachers relied heavily on these judgements in making important decisions relating to teaching approaches. The evidence suggests furthermore that the teachers found it possible and valuable to categorize pupils in these terms, especially those they saw as being at the extremes of the ability range, quite soon after they started teaching them; and that descriptions of pupils as more or less able tended to be quite firm and stable over time. Like other experienced teachers (see Berliner 1987), the teachers in this study relied heavily on their own observations in making judgements about their abilities. They showed themselves alert to pupils' greater strengths in some aspects of their subject work than in others, and especially to pupils' capacity to contribute well in oral work even when they were weak in literacy skills; but it was judgements of literacy skills and of work depending on such skills that seemed most to inform the generalized attributions of ability that were important to teachers.

The pressure on teachers to treat ability differences as fundamentally both unidimensional and stable clearly stems from their need to find ways of simplifying the complex task of managing the learning of all the pupils in their classrooms. Another basic way in which such simplifications can be achieved is through generally selecting tasks which can suitably be set in common for all the pupils in the classroom, and attending to differences among pupils only in so far as is possible within that common framework. Finding and fashioning such tasks is clearly a demanding business, and one very important aspect of how teachers went about it was through responding to pupils themselves in the kind of transactional patterns discussed in Chapter 6. It followed, however, that the nature of the tasks set for all often reflected the interests and felt needs of the most active and vocal members of classes.

As commentators, we have to raise the question of whether teachers' simplified ways of construing ability differences and their general use of common tasks for all pupils in their classes have serious costs for pupils' learning opportunities. However, given the complex differences between the pupils in any classroom, teachers have no option but to find ways of simplifying the task of catering for these differences. All ways of simplifying the task must have costs as well as benefits. For all the teachers who collaborated in this study, the benefits of setting common tasks for the whole class, and of treating ability differences as unidimensional and stable, seemed to outweigh the costs.

# 8 / *The crafts of the classroom*

In this final chapter we will review some of the major findings of our study and discuss their implications. In particular, we will focus on what we have learned about the ways in which the perceptions of the teachers and pupils in our study related to one another and how this knowledge might be used to enhance the effectiveness of teachers and schools. Our work can be taken to suggest that teachers can achieve a great deal in the classroom if they possess certain knowledge and skills. It also indicates, however, that what teachers are able to achieve is constrained by the context in which they have to work. It will be suggested that there may be important implications from this work for teachers in their everyday practice, as well as for teacher managers and those involved in the pre- and in-service training and education of teachers.

In relation to these intentions, it is important to sound a note of caution. All research studies have limitations. We believe a major strength of our study to be the depth and detail of the data we have gathered. Unfortunately, given the scarcity of resources available to support research of this kind, this richness was achieved at the expense of breadth of scale. We have studied a small group of teachers and pupils in one year group, and in only two subject areas. The problem of scale means that we must be extremely cautious in making generalizations based on this work. We do not know if a similar study of teachers and pupils in other subjects (e.g. science or maths) would have produced similar data. We have noted the influence that particular aspects of the National Curriculum orders had on teachers' thinking and actions, but we have no data on the effects of other curriculum areas on teachers' thinking and pupil experience. Similarly, we have not presented data concerning the thinking of teachers and pupils in other year groups, so we are not able to discuss the possible influence of age and stage factors. We have, since completing the study described here, been carrying out a similar study with year 9 pupils (aged 13–14 years), which will be reported at a later stage. Where generalizations from our present study are made they should be made in the form of hypotheses – very well grounded and substantiated, but still hypotheses only. Teachers and others may explore for themselves the validity of these hypotheses in relation to their own situations. We will finally, therefore, consider the possible shape of further studies that might develop from this work.

## Authenticity

Having stated these limitations, we should remind ourselves that this study has a firm methodological basis that gives us confidence in our findings as they stand. In building on the methodological foundations of the original study by Brown and McIntyre (1993), we have good grounds for believing that we obtained authentic accounts of teachers' and pupils' thinking about the issues in which we were interested. The combined force of the present study and the earlier work by Brown and McIntyre gives us confidence in the reliability of the methods used in these studies. This confidence is based in part on the richness of the accounts, and on the consistency within accounts and between accounts. We found, for example, a consistency in the ways in which teachers and pupils from different institutions talked about their classroom experience. We also found consistency between the same teachers' accounts taken at different times throughout the year. Likewise, pupils' accounts of their actions and thought processes were rich and detailed in ways that are unlikely to be fabricated. In particular, claims for authenticity are supported by the associations between pupil (and teacher) accounts and established theories of cognitive learning.

In addition, like Brown and McIntyre, we have faith that we created conditions that motivated the participants in our research to produce authentic accounts. We approached the teachers and pupils in this study from the point of view of seeking answers to the question: what is it that they do and think that helps them to be successful in promoting effective learning? Our focus on the positive, we believe, removed possible fear and suspicions that might have led to defensive and misleading responses. Furthermore, within the data, and through other communications with teachers and pupils we studied, we know that they found their involvement in this research valuable and rewarding in a practical sense, in that it helped them to articulate what was often tacit knowledge underlying their practice. This outcome was further underlined by the evident enthusiasm that the vast majority of participants showed in their engagement with the study – often exceeding the agreed time frames for interviews and volunteering insights and observations.

A valuable outcome of this study, then, is that it further validates the claim made by Brown and McIntyre (1993: 109) that it is possible, using the kinds of methods described here, to gain access to 'the substance and logic of teachers' professional craft knowledge'. We have also extended this claim by showing that similar methods can produce an equivalent understanding of pupils' thinking.

## The impact of the National Curriculum

A distinctive feature of the present study was that it took the unique opportunity to study teachers' and pupils' perceptions in the context of the introduction of the National Curriculum. It is perhaps unsurprising that the NC had a significant effect on the teachers in the present study, though the nature of some of these effects might not have been so predictable. Teachers' responses to it were complex and varied. For the most part teachers eschewed a straightforward implementation approach to the NC in favour of a critical and interpretive response. There were interesting individual differences in the degree to which teachers were prepared to challenge and deviate from the dictates of the NC. What was clear, however, was the way in which teachers saw themselves as having an active role in the construction of the curriculum as it is taught. The NC became an issue on which they focused their professional and scholarly knowledge about effective ways of teaching and about pupils' learning needs, as well as, in some cases, the knowledge they have derived as scholars in their teaching subjects. A striking feature of this aspect of the research was the sense of tension between teachers' views of themselves as active and critical professionals/scholars and the prescriptive qualities of the NC.

Furthermore, our findings suggested strongly not only that individual teachers' responses to the NC were influenced by the departmental context but also that in several cases the NC acted as a powerful catalyst to increase departmental influence on individuals. This was particularly the case in English, where prior to the NC a culture of individualism appears to have reigned within these departments. The advent of the NC brought with it, for some of these departments (both English and history), not only greater standardization in the content of their syllabi, but also greater interchange between teachers of methods of teaching. In this sense, therefore, one of the consequences of the NC was that it facilitated in some departments a focus on the craft knowledge of teaching, with the added benefit of helping some teachers to extend their existing knowledge into new areas of their subjects.

Having said this, we must reiterate the complexity of teachers' responses to the NC; for while there were reasons for welcoming the NC, these were mixed with reservations that were rooted in teachers' pragmatic and ideological concerns. These concerns meant that teachers were often selective in the ways in which they implemented the NC. There were also important differences between English and history. History teachers were generally positive about the rhetoric of the NC, but found that the content they saw themselves as obliged to cover forced them into significant and in their view undesirable changes in their teaching methods. English teachers generally responded favourably to the content of the NC but were often negative about the apparatus of attainment targets and levels and were conscious of what was felt as the looming threat of Key Stage 3 Standard Assessment Tasks.

It was in this context that we studied teachers' and pupils' craft knowledge.

## The crafts of the classroom

Brown and McIntyre's original research established a clear map of a group of teachers' general professional craft knowledge, in terms of their perceptions of classroom processes and outcomes. The research reported in this book took a narrower focus in seeking to uncover the thinking underpinning what teachers and pupils believed to be episodes of effective classroom *learning*. We wanted to find out about what teachers and pupils believed they did that was most helpful to them in their performance of activities that led to what they saw as effective pupil learning. We were particularly concerned with the ways in which answers to this question might be influenced by the context of the NC. Furthermore, we wanted to find out about teachers' ways of construing and responding to individual differences among pupils.

### Teachers' craft knowledge

Our study concurred with the earlier work of Brown and McIntyre (1993) in finding that teachers' craft knowledge about how to achieve desired goals was characterized by the need to take into account a wide range of sometimes competing factors. These included:

- the nature of the subject;
- pupil characteristics;
- their own knowledge and perceived abilities;
- the particular content being taught;
- time constraints;
- material conditions;

- the National Curriculum;
- departmental and school policy.

We also found, in relation to our distinctive concern with teaching that led to what teachers and pupils saw as effective learning, that teachers showed concern about their own specific performance and the ways in which this contributed to pupil learning in relation to short- and long-term learning objectives. These concerns were additional to the more short-term concerns identified as being of primary interest to the teachers in Brown and McIntyre's original work. Thus while the teachers in Brown and McIntyre's study evaluated lessons almost entirely in terms of pupil activities and progress, the teachers in the current study also showed a considerable readiness to talk about their own actions and thinking as they related to these activities. We speculate, on the basis of other evidence presented in this book, that these tendencies to talk spontaneously about longer-term learning objectives and about their own actions were, at least in part, attributable to the impact of the NC, both as a direct result of its overt emphasis on pupil attainment targets and levels, and indirectly through its impact on departmental discussion of teaching methods.

We must also point out that this difference may be related to the difference in emphasis between the two research studies. The particular focus on teaching leading to effective learning, as opposed to the more general notion of 'what went well from a teaching point of view', clearly focused teachers' thinking on one aspect of their craft knowledge. What is clear is that teachers in both studies construed 'teaching' in terms that were much wider than those aspects of teachers' activities that are calculated to lead to pupil learning. Such is the complexity of the teacher role and task, as construed by these teachers, that it is quite possible, and may even frequently be the case, that a lesson can be highly satisfactory from a teaching point of view when little or no subject learning has taken place at all. What is clear from the current study, however, is that where pupil learning of subject matter was the focus, these teachers placed a great deal of emphasis on their own performance in relation to that.

In relation to effective learning a distinctive feature of teachers' professional craft knowledge appears to have been a concern with pupil engagement. Teachers in this study placed a high value on strategies that stimulated pupils to be personally engaged with the lesson content. Thus strategies geared towards stimulating a positive affective response were sometimes of the same importance to teachers as strategies that had, primarily, a cognitive focus. Though there were occasions when teachers felt that it was necessary to prioritize affective or cognitive goals in order to achieve or maintain pupil engagement, a major priority among these teachers was to create circumstances in their classrooms that permitted pupils to perform as *active learners*.

*Pupils' craft knowledge*

We found that teachers and pupils possessed distinctive forms of craft knowledge that they employed in order to facilitate effective classroom learning. We observed that pupils generally showed a preference for certain teaching strategies and modes of engagement with teachers and learning tasks. The most effective teaching strategies and modes of engagement were characterized by the opportunities they created for pupils to make sense of the task *in their own terms*. This often involved 'concretization' processes, whereby subject matter was rendered accessible by being related to particular events, either imagined, as in a story, or actual, as in the experience of engaging in a role play or drama exercise. Visualization strategies were highly valued by many pupils. Sometimes illustrations and diagrams served this purpose. Other ways in which pupils actively worked to relate knowledge to their existing understandings involved collaborative and interactive methods, such as discussion, pair work and interchanges with the teacher, which created opportunities for knowledge to be presented and represented in different ways, with pupils actively seeking representations that were most personally meaningful. In these circumstances pupils would, for example, identify and store for future reference explanations modelled by peers or teachers.

Key features of pupil craft knowledge, therefore, were: (a) the identification of those methods of transformation best suited to their personal cognitive styles; (b) the identification of opportunities where they could engage with tasks in these preferred ways; and (c) the execution of their preferred styles. Teachers played an important role in the second of these features through their methods of presenting tasks to pupils. Teachers' modes of presentation in whole-class situations sometimes led to some pupils being catered for better than others. Furthermore, the social climate of the classroom, particularly in relation to the ways in which teachers related to pupils, was a significant factor for pupils, determining, in some cases, the degree to which they employed their most effective strategies or whether they chose to employ them at all. Our study focused on examples of perceived effective teaching and learning, but there is limited evidence to suggest that circumstances that pupils perceived to be socially and personally inimical were dealt with by pupils through the use of subtle avoidance strategies.

A particularly important factor affecting pupil engagement appears to have been related to individual differences between pupils. Pupils perceived to be of high ability sometimes expressed dissatisfaction with teaching methods that were welcomed by other pupils. The high ability pupils seemed to require more autonomy and less direct support than the teachers made available. On the other hand, pupils who were believed to have learning difficulties, particularly in relation to literacy skills, identified an over-reliance by teachers on literacy as a medium for learning and expression.

The importance of contextual factors in relation to pupil craft knowledge is highly significant. It forcibly mirrors an important aspect of teacher craft knowledge and, in so doing, underlines the systemic nature of craft knowledge. When we address issues of effectiveness in relation to teaching and learning, it soon becomes clear that we cannot discuss pupils' perceptions of effectiveness without reference to teachers' perceptions of effectiveness and vice versa.

### Teacher–pupil interactions

A major outcome of this study is the support it offers for a transactional theory of teaching and learning. We have shown that learning opportunities are felt by students and teachers to be heightened when teaching strategies are transactional, in that they involve the integration of pupil concerns and interests with teachers' pedagogical goals. It would also seem to be the case that opportunities for such transactional teaching may be limited by the presence of certain conditions, such as the requirement to prepare students for terminal examinations, particularly for those students who are perceived by their teachers to be of low ability.

The study has also highlighted the importance of teacher–student 'bi-directionality', which stresses the *interdependence* of teacher and student influence. A major way in which teachers facilitated the bi-directional process was through the use of interactive and reactive teaching strategies. Reactive and interactive teaching were distinguished by the extent to which teachers allowed lesson activities to be determined by their perceptions of student states or interests and the manner in which they allowed this to proceed. The employment of interactive or reactive approaches was constrained by individual differences between teachers, and by teachers' perceptions of specific conditions in which they were teaching, such as time and the NC.

What is important here is that the teachers and pupils in this study agreed that effective learning was most often associated with the teacher's willingness to allow students the space to engage with learning activities in their preferred ways, and to allow them to have influence on the selection of learning objectives; but that for teachers there are other dimensions to classroom teaching, including the need to take account of a multiplicity of contextual factors and of the differences among the pupils in the class.

### The importance of individual differences

An important aspect of effectiveness in relation to teaching and learning was that of individual differences between pupils. Teachers took particular actions on the basis of their perceptions of differences between pupils. The main ways in which teachers differentiated between pupils was in terms of pupil ability, behaviour and motivation, and personal attributes. It was noted that teachers developed stabilized typologies of pupils whom they believed to represent extremes of high or low ability quite early in their acquaintance with them. It was also shown that teachers catered for these differences through the use of individualized measures and group methods.

It is clear from this study that teachers placed a great deal of importance on their perceptions of differences between pupils, and that these perceptions in turn influenced their pedagogical decision-making and activities. It is also clear that pupils were affected by the decisions and actions that teachers took in this regard. There was a tendency, however, for teachers' methods of catering for these differences to have unwelcome consequences for some pupils. Thus, pupils who were perceived to be of high ability were sometimes frustrated by what they saw as the over directiveness of teachers. On the other hand, this over-directiveness was of clear benefit to apparently less able pupils. Furthermore, pupils who were perceived to be less able were disadvantaged by what teachers themselves sometimes saw as an unnecessary reliance on literacy skills as a medium for communication and learning.

For the most part, teachers sought to cater for individual differences within the framework of common tasks set by them for the whole class. In that teachers also tried as far as they considered it possible to be responsive to pupils' concerns and interests, it was to the class as a whole that they generally tried to be responsive; but this seemed to imply a greater responsiveness to those individuals who most actively participated in classroom talk with the teacher.

## Implications for teachers

These findings highlight the following issues that we believe to be significant to teachers.

Flexibility and responsiveness are important in teacher thinking. Teachers value their ability to think on their feet, and to adjust planned events to meet changing conditions. This places a stress on teacher opportunism in terms of seizing opportunities for capitalizing on opportunities that pupils present for effective teaching.

Crude prescriptions about 'good' and 'bad' teaching methods are inappropriate. The significant issue for the participants in this research was that of *goodness of fit*. Teachers were most satisfied with their teaching when they observed pupil behaviours that indicated appropriate engagement in learning tasks. They often accounted for these successes in terms of their complex and sophisticated management of lesson content and pupils.

There were some important common aspects of teaching that were perceived to be effective:

- clear goals for pupil learning;
- clarity of communication of lesson goals and agenda to pupils;
- use of preview and review of lesson content;
- helping pupils to contextualize content in terms of their own experience and knowledge, as well as in terms of other teaching goals and learning experiences;
- some willingness to allow pupils to have input into goal and agenda setting;
- supportive social context designed by teacher to help pupils feel accepted, cared for and valued;
- ability and willingness to allow for different cognitive styles and ways of engaging in the learning process among pupils, through multiple exemplification, the use of different types of illustration and mode of presentation, and offering pupils a choice from a menu of possible ways of engaging;
- willingness to take into account pupil circumstances and to modify/ pace/structure learning tasks accordingly.

It is important to intertwine affective and cognitive dimensions of teaching and learning. When teachers were explicit about this they revealed the high degree of skill and sophistication necessary for effective management of pupils and learning. Of particular importance here were consistent references to the need to create a positive social climate in the classroom, and the need for teaching approaches and learning tasks to be consistent with this endeavour.

The value and scope of pupil autonomy in classroom processes is also highlighted here. Common starting points in lessons do not have to lead to common tasks or common forms of pupil engagement. The differentiation process can be aided by informal peer tutoring and by encouraging pupils to reflect on their preferred forms of cognitive engagement.

Brown and McIntyre's study and the present study offer useful approaches through which teachers may be helped (for example, by colleagues) to articulate their craft knowledge. Teachers (and pupils) often surprised themselves with the depth and complexity of their insights into teaching and learning processes. Such articulation is clearly an aid to effective teaching (*and* learning), since it makes explicit, and therefore communicable, tacit knowledge. This is invaluable to the teacher for purposes of self-evaluation and professional development. It allows valuable insights to be passed on to colleagues and students. This also helps to combat the debilitating professional isolation that teachers often suffer. It also helps to draw attention to routine behaviours that have lost their value or have unexpected negative consequences.

The value of departmental (and interdepartmental) sharing of knowledge of effective teaching, as well as informal sharing of teaching approaches between staff, is evident.

Pupils are valuable as resources. The sophistication of pupil responses indicates that they are a vital source of useful information about their own learning processes and the ways in which contextual factors (classroom, task, peer and teacher variables) interact with these processes. There would appear to be a great deal of scope for pupil consultation that can be invaluable to teachers in their planning and execution of lessons. This, in turn, points to the value of engaging in pupil consultation in a variety of forms, such as casual oral enquiry, formal oral enquiry, observation of pupils and formal and informal written feedback.

## Implications for curriculum innovation

What can be learned about curriculum innovation from this study? What impact did the introduction of the NC have on teachers' professional craft knowledge. How if at all did the nature of teachers' craft knowledge influence the way in which the NC was received in schools? What implications are there for future practice?

It was difficult to predict in advance how the NC and teachers' existing practices would impinge on each other. Some predictions were very negative, from every point of view. Andy Hargreaves (1989), for example, thought that the NC would reinforce negative features of 'the culture of teaching', and also that the changes in classroom practice required for implementation of the NC would be actively resisted. On the basis of various studies of teachers over many years, he reasonably suggested that 'Teachers, it seems, are present-oriented, conservative and individualistic. They tend to avoid long-term planning and collaboration with their colleagues' (Hargreaves 1989: 27). These characteristics of the culture of teaching would, he suggested, be reinforced by the NC. Together with other government-inspired pressures and constraints, it would 'bind teachers ever more closely to the non-reflective immediacy of the classroom' (p. 38), and make it less possible for them to engage in systematic reflection of a critical and questioning kind. However, those promoting the NC should beware, because

> they are almost certainly also sowing seeds of failure and frustration in relation to their wider educational objectives. The culture of teaching can be as resistant to centrally imposed curricular initiatives as to any others. Where these initiatives call for substantial changes in classroom approach, the culture of teaching can supply powerful sources of classroom resistance.
>
> (Hargreaves 1989: 39)

As we have seen, to judge from our evidence these predictions turned out to be false in almost every respect. In most of the departments we studied, the NC has been an effective stimulus for collaborative planning and for the sharing of ideas among teachers. The contrast between Brown and McIntyre's findings and those of this study strongly suggest that the NC has also led teachers to take longer-term perspectives in considering their teaching and its effects. And while there was considerable diversity among teachers in their responses to innovative aspects of the NC, they tended generally to welcome both the definitive 'shape' that the NC offered for their subject and many of the specific extensions to their individual repertoires that the definition would imply.

While teachers' responses were thus far from conservative, neither were they uncritical or unquestioning. Almost all the teachers interviewed were fiercely, coherently and persuasively critical of some aspects of the NC. In history the weight of content, and in English the assessment arrangements, were general targets of criticism. But whatever was vague, arbitrary, mechanistic or internally inconsistent was critically questioned, as was anything seen to impose damaging constraints on classroom teaching and learning. As for the 'non-reflective immediacy of the classroom', again comparison with the Scottish results suggests that the NC has probably had a very significant impact in leading teachers to reflect on their own classroom practices.

Furthermore, the evidence gives very limited support to the idea of 'classroom resistance' to the NC. Certainly we have noted that teachers were often selective in their implementation of the NC. But even when it was against their better judgement, as was the case with history teachers under pressure to 'cover' content, most teachers tried to meet most of the requirements of the new curriculum. We have noted the tension between the prescriptions of the NC and teachers' views of themselves as scholarly professionals; but in general the tension was a productive one, with the NC being professionally interpreted, often at a departmental level, rather than being either explicitly rejected or implicitly resisted.

We could not have predicted in advance that the NC would be as well received as it was in the departments we studied, nor that it would have such apparently beneficial effects. In retrospect, then, what explanations are possible?

First, Hargreaves was correct that in important respects the NC was a conservative innovation. Not only was it, as he emphasized, academic and subject-based; it also, in both English and history, drew heavily on existing good practice in English schools. Here were not radical new ideas but rather the national seal of approval on, in English especially, a very catholic collection of ideas of good practice within the subject. The innovation was one of asking teachers within the subject to adopt each other's good ideas. Only the minority, with clearly articulated and strongly held subject ideologies, could object, and as we have seen they did so. (There were of course specific issues that were importantly contentious, but the great bulk of what was being proposed for each subject was already widely accepted.)

Second, adoption of the NC did not in itself directly require changes in classroom practice. Brown and McIntyre (1993: 116), in their discussion of curriculum innovation in relation to professional craft knowledge, note that 'many innovations are concerned with pupils' ways of working in classrooms, such as the nature of their talk, their practical activity, the sources of information they use, the ways they collaborate, the questions they seek to answer.' Others, they suggest, 'are concerned with teachers' use of accommodation, or resources, or time, with the ways they treat their subject matter, or the ways in which they deal with different pupils' (p. 117). Innovations of all these kinds, as they point out, have major implications for teachers' use of craft knowledge, involving the abandoning of well-developed practices and expertise and the learning of the new expertise necessary for the new approaches; and, they suggest, it is primarily because of the major costs implied for teachers in such changes that the adoption of externally initiated innovations is so rare. But the NC did not require such changes in teachers' normal practices. Most of the time, most teachers were able to go on using the same kinds of practices as those they were accustomed to using. Even for the history teachers, with their problems of content coverage, it was a matter of using accustomed methods more frequently than they would have chosen to use them. In so far as the NC put teachers under pressure to develop new craft knowledge, it was indirectly, so that they could teach appropriately for specified learning objectives; and it was as *extensions* of existing repertoires, and generally extensions that could be developed through following plans and advice from departmental colleagues accustomed to using these approaches.

Related to this is a third factor. It became very clear that both the quality of NC implementation in a department and the extent to which advantage was taken of the NC for the professional development of teachers depended substantially on the extent to which the department responded to it *corporately*; and that, in turn, depended largely on the leadership provided by the head of department. Readiness by heads of department not simply to accept the NC, but rather to use it as a stimulus for departmental exchanges of ideas and as a framework within which the strengths of different members of staff could be recognized and used, was an important factor in generating the generally positive outcomes we observed.

Fourth, it seemed that the NC frameworks of attainment targets and statements of attainment for different levels, although not in themselves much admired, or even very much studied in some departments, did have the effect of encouraging teachers to think more about what they wanted their pupils to learn, both in the short term and in the longer term. It seemed that the NC's explicit emphasis on what pupils should learn had an important influence on teachers' own agendas, and led them to think much more explicitly about the learning to which their teaching was directed than was the case for teachers in other studies, such as that of Brown and McIntyre (1993).

Finally, it would be wrong to underemphasize the importance of the simple fact that the NC was understood by teachers not as an option but as a legal obligation. Hargreaves (1989) greatly overstated his case in suggesting that 'the culture of teaching can be as resistant to centrally imposed curricular innovations as to any others.' The teachers with whom we worked took the NC very seriously. They recognized that their pupils, and ultimately they themselves, would be judged in relation to the content and the attainment criteria of the NC; and while that in itself is far from a sufficient explanation for their collaboration with the NC, it certainly gave it a cutting edge which would otherwise have been absent.

We would draw two lessons from the above analysis.

1 Centrally imposed curriculum innovations can be very effective where:
   (a) they are concerned to make more generally available good practices which are already widely accepted within the relevant body of teachers;
   (b) there are people in the schools who have the right positions, the commitment and the ability to manage sensitively the effective implementation of the innovations.
2 Externally generated innovations in teaching are much more likely to succeed if they are formulated not in terms of changes in classroom practice, but instead in terms of subject content and of learning objectives, and if in addition teachers have available to them examples of other teachers, working in circumstances like their own, whose classroom practice is concerned with the innovative content and is directed towards the innovative learning objectives.

## Implications for initial teacher education

One of the greatest difficulties for student-teachers in learning how to teach is that they mistake the nature of the task. It is easy for them to believe that successful teaching depends on having the right recipes, together with an appropriate personality and established status. They need to learn instead that successful teaching depends on the kind of flexible responsiveness to pupils and to other circumstances manifested by the teachers we studied and thus on developing a sophisticated and fluently used professional craft knowledge.

That is a lesson which is best learned through access to the craft knowledge of known and respected individual teachers; but that is not something that is achieved through conventional approaches to observation and supervision. Brown and McIntyre (1993) suggested tentatively that as far as possible student-teachers should adopt the same procedures for getting access to teachers' craft knowledge that they had successfully used in their research. Recent research at Oxford (Hagger 1995) has fully confirmed the validity of this suggestion: if student-teachers focus their questions to teachers whose lessons they have observed on specific successful aspects of those lessons, and seek teachers' explanations of these successful actions or of the successful outcomes, they are very likely to gain access to rich accounts of the teachers' craft knowledge.

At different stages in their initial professional education, student-teachers need to gain access to different facets of teachers' craft knowledge. At the beginning, it is just getting a general sense of the nature of this knowledge and of teachers' expertise that is important: there is little point in the extensive early observation that student-teachers are generally asked to engage in unless the observed teachers can afterwards explain in some detail what they were doing and why.

One particular facet of teachers' craft knowledge to which student-teachers could very usefully gain access is that concerned with classroom management and control. For many student-teachers, the nature of appropriate teacher–pupil relationships is a source of confusion and stress, with early images of pupils responding appreciatively to teacher friendliness tending to give way to obsessive concern with classroom control. In this book we have highlighted the way in which teachers' actions tend to be guided by the interacting concerns for the achievement of cognitive objectives, for a positive and caring classroom climate, for such other affective objectives as pupils' enjoyment of the subject and for classroom control. Given access to such craft knowledge, student-teachers would learn, perhaps more quickly than they often do, that success depends on being able, cleverly and thoughtfully, to pick the path which maximizes the achievement of all these objectives, and on judging which of them has to be given priority at any particular time. The learning would be much less stressful if it were recognized early as the learning of very difficult skills, not a matter of adopting strong positions or having an appropriate personality.

We emphasize experienced teachers' craft knowledge as a major resource in initial teacher education because it has for so long been neglected. Student-teachers should not, however, be encouraged to accept the authority of such craft knowledge without question. For a start, individual teachers' craft knowledge is demonstrably idiosyncratic: no two teachers have the same repertoires, use the same criteria or take account of the same range of factors in making judgements. More fundamentally, it must be remembered that teachers have developed their craft knowledge pragmatically and intuitively in response to the pressing demands of classroom life; and they themselves have generally not articulated it clearly enough to examine it critically. Before student-teachers choose to make such knowledge their own, *they* need to examine it critically.

The importance of such critical examination of craft knowledge is reflected in our finding – perhaps the most important reported in this book – of the very different judgements that teachers and pupils make about effective classroom teaching for learning. The pupils offer some quite straightforward prescriptions for the kind of teaching that will facilitate their learning. Teachers, on the other hand, while broadly endorsing pupils' judgements, treat classroom teaching as a much less straightforward business, in which many more things need to be taken into account. Pupils quite clearly do not understand the complexity of classroom teaching from a teacher's perspective, and it can be tempting to dismiss their views as naive and egocentric. On the other hand, the *raison d'être* of classroom activity *is* to promote pupils' learning; and it is just possible that teachers, overwhelmed by the multiplicity of things they need to attend to, including the diversity of pupils in their classes, and the diverse social and affective as well as cognitive goals with which they need to be concerned, might sometimes in practice lose sight of the priority they should be giving to pupils' learning. At the very least, pupils' perspectives on what helps them to learn in classrooms can provide one valuable touchstone against which student-teachers can examine experienced teachers' professional craft knowledge.

Such valuing of the ideas from one source that might usefully guide one's practice, at the same time subjecting these ideas to critical examination in the light of ideas from a different source, is exactly the kind of 'practical theorizing' approach to teacher education that we have been seeking to develop at Oxford University in recent years (e.g. McIntyre 1990, 1995). The professional craft knowledge of teachers is particularly valued as an enormously rich source of practical wisdom (practicality having been an undervalued concern in teacher education in earlier decades, just as wisdom is in danger of being undervalued currently). But ideas from teachers' craft knowledge do need to be examined carefully in terms of their clarity, their coherence, their generalizability and their implicit values and assumptions. These ideas also need to be supplemented, sometimes to be reinforced and sometimes to be challenged, by ideas for practice from a variety of other sources, such as pupils, research of the kind reported here or psychologists like Bruner and Vygotsky, to whose work we referred in Chapter 6. The divergence between the valuable insights of teachers and those of pupils that we have reported exemplifies very well the need for student-teachers to be pressed, and to be helped, to look critically at all ideas for practice, whatever their source.

**Implications for schools' and teachers' development**

What does this research tell us about ways in which schools can develop themselves, and help their teachers to develop, to become more effective in promoting pupils' learning? We hope first of all that it is an effective reminder of the fact that it is *in classrooms* that pupils do nearly all their school learning, and that the task of effectively fostering that learning demands from teachers great energy, sensitivity and most of all sophisticated expertise. Senior management teams sometimes seem to forget that *their* usefulness depends primarily on how successful they are at appreciating, supporting and facilitating the work that teachers do in classrooms. Serious school development *means* helping teachers to develop the quality of their classroom teaching.

Second, our research leads to a number of conclusions that strongly overlap with conclusions reached by Brown and McIntyre (1993) and that may be summarized as follows.

- Research on teachers' craft knowledge provides, in both its procedures and its findings, a clear alternative to the 'deficit model' of teachers on which in-service education has conventionally been based, and which has led to much of that in-service education being very ineffective.
- 'A productive way to open teachers' classroom doors to one another is through observers firmly committing themselves both to an exclusively positive view of what they observe and to understanding events from the perspective of the observed teacher' (Brown and McIntyre 1993: 115).
- All experienced teachers can benefit through a sharing of their classroom expertise with one another: there is *within* almost all schools a rich reservoir of teaching expertise on which much useful in-service teacher education could be based.
- When teachers have begun to make their craft knowledge explicit, and have as a result developed confidence about the quality of expertise embedded in their day-to-day practice, they are enabled and encouraged to subject that practice to critical examination.
- For effective appraisal of classroom teaching, it is both necessary and possible for the observed teacher to explain to the observer, however experienced that observer is, what he or she has been doing in the observed teaching. Teachers are able, when treated respectfully and asked appropriate questions in a reflective atmosphere, to provide clear and valid explanations of this kind, and observers' understanding of the observed teaching depends on such explanations.
- 'To get a reliable and valid picture of any one teacher's strengths, it is necessary to learn about that teacher's teaching of different kinds of lessons to different classes in different circumstances' (Brown and McIntyre 1993: 119). Except in extreme cases, appraisal of teachers'

classroom teaching is a realistic enterprise only if the teachers being appraised are given responsibility for both the agenda to be pursued and the selection of occasions on which they are observed.

Third, just as the two research projects have, in their findings and in their procedures, suggested fruitful ways in which teachers can be helped to articulate the craft knowledge hitherto implicit in their practice, and thence take pride in it, share it and reflect critically upon it, so, we believe, this second project suggests ways in which pupils could fruitfully contribute to school and teacher development. It is not only, or even primarily, in their feedback to their own teachers that pupils can contribute. We suspect that hearing directly from pupils about how their learning has been facilitated by other teachers could be a powerful stimulus to teachers in encouraging them to extend, and perhaps to reflect on, their own teaching repertoires.

Fourth, our research findings strongly suggest that school development to improve pupils' classroom learning can usefully be thought of in terms of two complementary kinds of strategy. The first of these, on which we have concentrated so far, is concerned with helping teachers to develop their classroom teaching expertise. The other kind of strategy, which perhaps might receive more attention than it generally does, is concerned with minimizing the constraints upon teachers' opportunities to foster effective learning in their classrooms. We are of course referring back here to the fairly strong consensus found between teachers and pupils about what leads to effective learning, and to the fact that teachers' practices none the less diverged considerably from these consensus ideas because of the many other factors by which they were constrained. Some of these factors are of course implicit in the system of classroom teaching. Others are a direct consequence of National Curriculum and assessment requirements. Many, however, are potentially within the control of individual schools.

A crucial set of constraints relate to the general ethos of the school: the individual teacher's task is made more difficult if there is not a school climate in which all individuals are consistently treated with respect, in which pupils have a sense of mutual obligation to each other, in which successful learning is seen as what the school is about and in which there are high expectations for the success of all. Among other things that can impose important constraints upon teachers are: accommodation; the availability, good working order and number of items of equipment, materials and books; the size and composition of classes; timetabling; interruptions to teaching; pupil lateness and absence; and internal school arrangements for examinations. It is not suggested that any of these constraints can be easily dealt with. What is suggested is that school development plans should in large measure be concerned with the minimization of such constraints on classroom teaching for learning, and that just as teachers need to listen to their pupils, so school managements and governors need to listen to their teachers in order to identify the most serious of the constraints.

Finally, during the course of this research project, an increasingly important concern for schools in England has been the need to prepare for, submit to and take account of school inspections under the auspices of the Office for Standards in Education (OFSTED). These inspections are on the one hand stressful, time-consuming and disruptive for schools but, on the other hand, they are potentially valuable for both accountability and school development purposes. We mention them here for two related reasons. First, much of the time of inspection teams, under Ofsted rules, is devoted to observation in classrooms, and this observation is used as a major source of the evidence on which reports are based. Second, in draft proposals for a modified framework for inspections, it is suggested that inspectors should take greater account of schools' own agendas, and especially their development plans. This would indeed be welcome, but we would suggest that a basic first step in that direction must be for all classroom observation to be followed by unhurried discussion in a quiet setting about the lesson with the observed teacher. Judgements of the quality of observed teaching that do not take account of the intentions, perceptions and decisions of the teachers (far less of the pupils) can claim very little validity, for either accountability or developmental purposes. For inspectors to claim, without such consultation, to understand what has happened, and to go on to make inferences about what *ought* to have happened, means that the whole exercise can have very little credibility.

## Conclusion

In this book we have reported our attempts to extend the exploration of teachers' professional craft knowledge in a number of directions. In doing so, we have found that in many respects the earlier Scottish findings of Brown and McIntyre (1993) are generalizable to the context of year 7 English and history teaching within the framework of the National Curriculum in England. In other respects, this distinctive context does seem to have had a significant impact on the thinking underlying teachers' everyday practice. Our research has focused especially on teachers' efforts to foster pupils' subject learning and on the ways in which they take account of differences among pupils; and perhaps the most important part of our work has been to explore pupils' own accounts of their learning, and to relate these to teachers' accounts. We are conscious, however, of still being in the very early stages of this work. In particular, the generalizability of *our* findings, for example to different subjects, different age groups and different curriculum and cultural contexts, now needs to be examined. We ourselves are currently engaged in analysing our research findings with regard to year 9 English and history teaching and learning in the National Curriculum context, and the difference in age groups does seem to have some significant implications. What does seem beyond question is the complexity and the variety of the teaching and learning crafts of the classroom.

# References

Baddeley, A. (1990). *Human Memory: Theory and Practice*, London: Allyn and Bacon.

Ball, S. (1985). 'Participant observation with pupils'. In R. Burgess (ed.) *Strategies of Educational Research: Qualitative Methods*, Lewes: Falmer Press.

Ball, S. and Bowe, R. (1991). 'Subject to change? Subject departments and the "implementation" of national curriculum policy: an overview of the issues'. Centre for Educational Studies, King's College London.

Barnes, A. (1993). 'Pioneers of practice', *Times Educational Supplement (English Extra)*, 5 March, 4.

Barnes, D. (1976). *From Communication to Curriculum*, Harmondsworth: Penguin.

Ben-Peretz, M., Bromme, R. and Halkes, R. (eds) (1986). *Advances of Research on Teacher Thinking*, Lisse: Swets and Zeilinger.

Bennett, N., Desforges, C., Cockburn, A. and Wilkinson, B. (1984). *The Quality of Pupil Learning Experiences*, London: Lawrence Erlbaum Associates.

Berliner, D.C. (1987). 'Ways of thinking about students and classrooms by more and less experienced teachers'. In J. Calderhead (ed.) *Exploring Teachers' Thinking*, London: Cassell.

Biggs, J. (1987). 'Student approaches to learning and studying', *British Journal of Educational Psychology*, 63, 1–19.

Bloom, B.S. (1977). *Human Characteristics and School Learning*, New York: McGraw-Hill.

Brophy, J. (ed.) (1991). *Advances in Research on Teaching, Volume 2*, Greenwich, CT: JAI Press.

Brophy, J. and Good, T. (1986). 'Teacher behaviour and pupil achievement'. In M. Wittrock (ed.) *Handbook of Research on Teaching*, 3rd edn, London: Macmillan.

Brown, S. and McIntyre, D. (1993). *Making Sense of Teaching*, Buckingham: Open University Press.

Bruner, J. (1987). 'The transactional self'. In J. Bruner and H. Haste (eds) *Making Sense: the Child's Construction of the World*, London: Methuen.

Bruner, J. and Haste, H. (1987). *Making Sense: the Child's Construction of the World*, London: Methuen.

Calderhead, J. (ed.) (1987). *Exploring Teachers' Thinking*, London: Cassell.

Calderhead, J. (ed.) (1988). *Teachers' Professional Learning*, Lewes: Falmer Press.

Carter, K. (1990). 'Teachers' knowledge and learning to teach'. In W.R. Houston (ed.) *Handbook of Research on Teacher Education*, New York: Macmillan.

Clandinin, J. (1986). *Classroom Practice: Teachers' Images in Action*, London: Falmer Press.

Clark, C. (1986). 'Ten years of conceptual development in research on teachers' thinking'. In M. Ben-Peretz *et al.* (eds) *Advances of Research on Teacher Thinking*, Lisse: Swets and Zeilinger.

Clark, C. and Peterson, P. (1986). 'Teachers' thought processes'. In M. Wittrock (ed.) *Handbook of Research on Teaching*, London: Macmillan.

Cohen, D. (1977). *Ideas and Action: Social Science and Craft in Educational Practice*, Chicago: Center for New Schools.

Coleman, J.S., Campbell, E.Q., Hobson, C.J., McPartland, J., Mood, A.A., Weinfeld, F.S. and York, R.L. (1966). *Equality of Educational Opportunity (Report from the Office of Education)*, Washington, DC: US Government Printing Office.

Collicott, S. (1990). 'Who is the national history curriculum for?', *Teaching History*, October, 8–12.

Cooper, H. (1983). 'Communication of teacher expectations to students'. In J. Levine and M. Wang (eds) *Teacher and Student Perceptions: Implications for Learning*, London: ILEA.

Cooper, H.M. and Good, T.L. (1982). *Pygmalion Grows up: Studies in the Expectation Communication Process*, New York: Longman.

Cooper, P. (1989). 'Respite, relationships and resignification: the effects of residential schooling on pupils with emotional and behavioural difficulties with particular reference to the pupil perspective', unpublished PhD thesis. Birmingham University.

Cooper, P. (1993a). *Effective Schools for Disaffective Students*, London: Routledge.

Cooper, P. (1993b). 'Exploring pupils' perceptions of residential schooling for children within emotional and behavioural difficulties', *Child and Youth Care Forum*, 22, 2.

Cooper, P. (1993c). 'Learning from the pupil perspective', *British Journal of Special Education*, 20, 4.

Cooper, P. (1993d). 'Field relations and the problem of authenticity in researching participants' perceptions of teaching and learning in classrooms', *British Educational Research Journal*, 19(4), 323–38.

Cooper, P. and McIntyre, D. (1993). 'Commonality in teachers' and pupils' perceptions of effective classroom learning', *British Journal of Educational Psychology*, 63, 381–99.

Cooper, P. and McIntyre, D. (1994a). 'Patterns of interaction between teachers' and pupils' classroom thinking and their implications for the provision of learning opportunities in classrooms'. Paper presented at the annual meeting of the American Educational Research Association, New Orleans, April.

Cooper, P. and McIntyre, D. (1994b). 'Teachers' and pupils' perceptions of effective classroom learning: conflicts and commonalities'. In M. Hughes (ed.) *Perceptions of Teaching and Learning*, Clevedon: Multilingual Matters.

Cooper, P. and McIntyre, D. (1995). 'The importance of power sharing in classrooms'. In M. Hughes (ed.) *Teaching and Learning in Changing Times*, Oxford: Blackwell.

Corno, L. and Snow, R.E. (1986). 'Adapting teaching to individual differences among learners'. In M.C. Wittrock (ed.) *Handbook of Research on Teaching, Third Edition*, New York: Macmillan.

Dahllof, U. and Lundgren, U. (1970). 'Macro and micro approaches combined for curriculum process analysis: a Swedish educational field project'. Institute of Education, University of Gothenburg.

Day, C., Calderhead, J. and Denicolo, P. (1993). *Research on Teacher Thinking: Understanding Professional Development*, London: Falmer Press.

Day, C., Pope, M. and Denicolo, P. (1990). *Insights into Teachers' Thinking and Practice*, Basingstoke: Falmer Press.

Desforges, C. and McNamara, D. (1977). 'One man's heuristic is another man's blindfold: some comments on applying social science to educational practice', *British Journal of Teacher Education*, 3(1), 27–39.

Desforges, C. and McNamara, D. (1979). 'Theory and practice: methodological procedures for the objectification of craft knowledge', *British Journal of Teacher Education*, 5(2), 145–52.

Dweck, C.S., Davidson, W., Nelson, S. and Enna, B. (1978). 'Sex differences in learned helplessness. 2, The contingencies of evaluative feedback in the classroom. 3, An experimental analysis', *Developmental Psychology*, 14, 268–76.

Ebel, K.E. (1976). *The Craft of Teaching: a Guide to Mastering the Professor's Art*, San Francisco: Jossey Bass.

Eisner, E. (1985). *The Educational Imagination*, London: Macmillan.

Elbaz, F. (1981). 'Teachers' practical knowledge, report of a case study', *Curriculum Inquiry*, 11(1), 43–7.

Elbaz, E. (1983). *Teacher Thinking: a Study of Practical Knowledge*, London: Croom Helm.

Hackman, S. (1993). 'The age of conformity', *Times Educational Supplement* (*English Extra*), 5 March, 1.

Hagger, H. (1995). 'The problems and possibilities for student-teachers of gaining access to experienced teachers' professional craft knowledge'. Thesis submitted for the degree of Doctor of Philosophy at the University of Oxford.

Halkes, R. and Olson, J. (eds) (1984). *Teacher Thinking*, Lisse: Swets and Zeilinger.

Hammersley, M. and Atkinson, P. (1983). *Ethnography: Principles in Practice*, London: Routledge.

Hargreaves, A. (1989). 'Curriculum policy and the culture of teaching'. In G.M. Iburn, I.F. Goodson and R.J. Clark (eds) *Re-interpreting Curriculum Research: Images and Arguments*, London: Falmer Press.

Hargreaves, D., Hester, S. and Mellor, F. (1975). *Deviance in Classrooms*, London: Routledge.

Her Majesty's Inspectorate (1978). *Mixed Ability Work in Comprehensive Schools*, London: HMSO.

Keddie, N. (1971). 'Classroom knowledge'. In M. Young (ed.) *Knowledge and Control*, London: Collier Macmillan.

Leinhardt, G., Putnam, R.T., Stein, M.K. and Baxter, J. (1991). 'Where subject knowledge matters'. In J. Brophy (ed.) *Advances in Research on Teaching, Volume 2*, Greenwich, CT: JAI Press.

Lepper, M. (1983). 'Extrinsic reward and intrinsic motivation: implications for the classroom'. In J. Levine and M. Wang (eds) *Teacher and Student Perceptions: Implications for Learning*, London: ILEA.

Levine, J. and Wang, M. (eds) (1983). *Teacher and Student Perceptions: Implications for Learning*, London: ILEA.

Little, V. (1990). 'A national curriculum in history: a very contentious issue', *British Journal of Educational Studies*, 38(4), 319–34.

Logan, T. (1984). 'Learning through interviewing'. In J. Schostak and T. Logan (eds) *Pupil Experience*, London: Croom Helm.

Lortie, D.C. (1975). *Schoolteacher: a Sociological Study*, Chicago: University of Chicago Press.

McArthur, T. (1993). 'Language used as a loaded gun', *Guardian Education*, 20 April, 3.

McIntyre, D. (1990). 'Ideas and principles guiding the internship scheme'. In P. Benton (ed.) *The Oxford Internship Scheme*, London: Calouste Gulbenkian Foundation.

McIntyre, D. (1995). 'In defence of a practical theorising approach to initial teacher education', *British Journal of Educational Studies*, 43, 4.

McNamara, D. and Desforges, C. (1978). 'The social sciences, teacher education and the objectification of craft knowledge', *British Journal of Teacher Education*, 4(1), 17–36.

Marks, R. (1990). 'Pedagogical content knowledge: from a mathematical case to a modified conception', *Journal of Teacher Education*, 41(3), 3–11.

Newbold, D. (1977). *Ability Grouping: The Hanbury Enquiry*, Slough: NFER.

Nisbett, R. and Wilson, T. (1977). 'Telling more than we can know: verbal reports as data', *Psychological Review*, 84(3), 231–59.

Pendry, A. (1994). 'The pre-lesson pedagogical decision-making of history student-teachers during the internship year'. Thesis submitted for the degree of Doctor of Philosophy at the University of Oxford.

Peterson, P.L. and Swing, S.R. (1982). 'Beyond time on task: students' reports of their thought processes during direct instruction', *Elementary School Journal*, 82, 481–91.

Postlethwaite, K. and Denton, C. (1978). *Streams for the Future?* Slough: NFER.

Powney, J. and Watts, M. (1987). *Interviewing in Educational Research*, London: Routledge.

Reid, M., Clunies-Ross, L., Goacher, B. and Vile, C. (1981). *Mixed Ability Teaching: Problems and Possibilities*, Windsor: NFER/Nelson.

Rogers, C. (1951). *Client Centred Therapy*, London: Constable.

Rogers, C. (1980). *A Way of Being*, Boston: Houghton Mifflin.

Roy, D. (1991). 'Improving recall by eyewitnesses through the cognitive interview', *The Psychologist*, 14(9), 398–400.

Schön, D.A. (1983). *The Reflective Practitioner*, London: Temple Smith.

Schön, D.A. (1987). *Educating the Reflective Practitioner*, London: Jossey Bass.

Schunk, D. and Meece, J. (eds) (1992). *Student Perceptions in the Classroom*, New Jersey: LEA.

Shavelson, R., Webb, N. and Burstein, L. (1986). 'Measurement of teaching'. In M. Wittrock (ed.) *Handbook of Research on Teaching*, London: Macmillan.

Shulman, L. (1986). 'Paradigms and research programmes in the study of teaching'. In M. Wittrock (ed.) *Handbook of Research on Teaching*, London: Macmillan.

Simpson, M. (1989). *A Study of Differentiation and Learning in Schools*, Aberdeen: Northern College.

Slater, J. (1991). 'History in the national curriculum: the final report of the history working group'. In R. Aldrich (ed.) *History in the National Curriculum*, London, Kogan Page and the London University Institute of Education.

Slavin, R.E. (1983). *Co-operative Learning*, New York: Longman.

Slavin, R.E. (1987). 'Ability grouping and student achievement in elementary schools: a best-evidence synthesis', *Review of Educational Research*, 57(3), 293–336.

Slavin, R.E. (1990). 'Achievement effects of ability grouping in secondary schools: a best evidence synthesis', *Review of Educational Research*, 60(3), 471–500.

Tesch, R. (1990). *Qualitative Research: Analysis Types and Software Tools*, Lewes: Falmer.

Tom, A. (1984). *Teaching as a Moral Craft*, New York: Longman.

Vygotsky, L. (1987). *The Collected Works of L. S. Vygotsky, Volume 1*, London: Plenum.

Wang, M. (1983). 'Development and consequences of students' sense of personal control'. In J. Levine and M. Wang (eds) *Teacher and Student Perceptions: Implications for Learning*, London: ILEA.

Wang, M. (1990). 'The learning characteristics of learning disabled students'. In M. Wang (ed.) *Special Education, Research and Practice*, Oxford: Pergamon.

Wang, M.C. and Palincsar, A.S. (1989). 'Teaching students to assume an active role in their learning'. In M.C. Reynolds (ed.) *Knowledge Base for the Beginning Teacher*, Oxford: Pergamon.

Wang, M. and Walberg, H. (1983). 'Evaluating educational programmes', *Educational Evaluation and Policy Analysis*, 5, 347–66.

Webb, N.M. (1983). 'Predicting learning from student interaction: defining the interaction variables', *Educational Psychologist*, 18, 33–42.

Weinstein, C.F. and Mayer, R.F. (1986). 'The teaching of learning strategies'. In M.C. Wittrock (ed.) *Handbook of Research on Teaching*, 3rd edn, London: Macmillan.

Weinstein, R. (1986). 'Students' perceptions of schooling', *Elementary School Journal*, 83(4), 297–312.

Wilson, S., Shulman, L. and Rickert, A. (1987). '150 ways of knowing: representations of knowledge in teaching'. In J. Calderhead (ed.) *Exploring Teachers' Thinking*, London: Cassell.

Wittrock, M.C. (1986). 'Students thought processes'. In M.C. Wittrock (ed.) *Handbook of Research on Teaching*, 3rd edn, London: Macmillan.

Woods, P. (1990). *The Happiest Days? How Pupils Cope with School*, London: Falmer Press.

# Author index

# Subject index

# MAKING SENSE OF TEACHING

## Sally Brown and Donald McIntyre

This book helps us to understand better the nature of teaching in schools and, in particular, to understand teaching from the perspective of the people doing it: the teachers. The authors seek to gain access to teachers' professional craft knowledge and to facilitate teachers' own articulation of the ordinary, everyday teaching which they do routinely and spontaneously in classrooms. Their emphasis throughout is on investigating 'good teaching', on what does well in the classroom. They are also concerned to identify how an understanding of the professional craft knowledge of teachers is particularly important for, and applicable to, the preservice and inservice training of teachers, effective curriculum innovation, and teacher appraisal. They help us to make sense of what goes on in good teaching, and draw out the significant implications for policy and practice.

> This is an admirable, much needed book that I can not recommend too highly to anyone involved in teaching or teacher education at any level. I am sure that it will inspire all its readers to reflect more on their own teaching and, hopefully, become involved in similar investigations.
> (*British Journal of Educational Technology*)

## Contents
*Making sense of teaching: a priority for theory, policy and practice – Identifying 'good teaching' – How do teachers talk about their good teaching? – Generalizations across teachers: goals and actions – The conditions of teaching and a theoretical framework – The routines teachers use to achieve their goals – Making sense of teaching: conclusions and implications – References – Index.*

144pp      0 335 15795 5 (Paperback)      0 335 15796 3 (Hardback)

## TEACHERS TALK ABOUT TEACHING:
## COPING WITH CHANGE IN TURBULENT TIMES

**Judith Bell (ed.)**

This book considers the impact of some of the far-reaching educational reforms introduced in the UK during the last decade, from the point of view of those people who have been required to implement them. All the contributors are, or were, teachers and all are committed to providing the best possible education for school students. Their views on the impact of some of the reforms provide an insight into what it is like to work in schools today and the effect the many demands placed on them have had on their lives. They consider the impact of the National Curriculum (and the associated methods of assessment), career prospects, appraisal, the changed role of governors, the influence of Local Management of Schools and the low morale of many teachers. Throughout the book, the unifying threads are how teachers are coping with change and ways in which their interpretation of autonomy and professionalism differ from those of some ministers and administrators. These messages from the 'coalface' are worthy of serious consideration by all who have a concern for quality education and for the well-being of learners and teachers alike.

### Contents
*Introduction – PART 1: Changing teaching: Teachers coping with change – Teachers out of control – Teachers autonomy under siege? – PART 2: Careering teachers: New to teaching – In mid-career – From middle to senior management – Leaving the profession – Revisiting classrooms – PART 3: Moving to local management: Not all plain sailing – Governors and teachers: the costs of LMS – PART 4: Subject to change: Careers education: the fight for recognition – At the Core: 'Oh to be in England!' – Postscript – References – Index.*

### Contributors
Judith Bell, Ken Bryan, Rosemary Chapman, Karen Cowley, Ann Hanson, Jill Horder, Gill Richardson, John Ross, Andrew Spencer, Peter Swientozielskyj, Lorna Unwin, Stephen Waters.

144pp      0 335 19174 6      (Paperback)